IMAGES OF WAR
ANIMALS IN
THE GREAT WAR

RARE PHOTOGRAPHS FROM WARTIME ARCHIVES

IMAGES OF WAR
ANIMALS IN THE GREAT WAR

RARE PHOTOGRAPHS FROM WARTIME ARCHIVES

LUCINDA MOORE

Pen & Sword
MILITARY

First published in Great Britain in 2017 by
PEN & SWORD MILITARY
an imprint of
Pen and Sword Books Ltd
47 Church Street
Barnsley
South Yorkshire S70 2AS

ISBN 978 1 47386 211 1

Printed and bound in Malta by Gutenberg Press Ltd.

Pen & Sword Books Ltd incorporates the imprints of Pen & Sword Archaeology, Atlas, Aviation, Battleground, Discovery, Family History, History, Maritime, Military, Naval, Politics, Railways, Select, Social History, Transport, True Crime, and Claymore Press, Frontline Books, Leo Cooper, Praetorian Press, Remember When, Seaforth Publishing and Wharncliffe.

For a complete list of Pen and Sword titles please contact
Pen and Sword Books Limited
47 Church Street, Barnsley, South Yorkshire, S70 2AS, England
E-mail: enquiries@pen-and-sword.co.uk
Website: www.pen-and-sword.co.uk

Contents

Introduction

Though in no way intended as a complete history of animals in the Great War, this book aims to throw a spotlight on the many ways in which creatures, great and small, were affected by the First World War, and also the ways in which those creatures contributed to the war effort. Their stories are told through the lens of original archival material from the Mary Evans Picture Library, through privileged access to the lushly illustrated wartime periodicals and other publications from the era.

Rescue of Norah the bulldog mascot and the ship's pets after the sinking of HMS *King Edward VII* in January 1916.

Chapter 1

Tails from the sea

As part of the theatre of war, the sea was a backdrop to a remarkable variety of animals, aquatic and otherwise. Through the visual material held in the Mary Evans Picture Library, the lesser known stories of these creatures who lived above and beneath the ocean waves can be told.

The depiction opposite by Italian artist Cyrus Cuneo in the children's book *Great Deeds of the Great War* shows the rescue of the ship's pets after the sinking of HMS *King Edward VII* in January 1916. The ship struck a drifting mine off the coast of Cape Wrath, Scotland, and was badly damaged in the explosion. Some crew members courageously risked their lives to round up the ship's menagerie of pets as the vessel began to sink. Able Seaman Needham is pictured placing Norah the bulldog, the ship's mascot, into a lifeboat that was already being lowered. Besides Norah, the ships' two monkeys were rescued by Leading Seaman Wood; no mean feat, as they were reportedly in a state of considerable agitation after the explosion, and scampering about wildly. The ship's parrot was not used to being manhandled, had to be set free, and was last seen heading in the direction of shore. The men hunted fruitlessly for the ship's three cats as the vessel sank further into the water, though eventually two kittens were discovered. One had run into one of the ship's guns, and could not be removed in time, but the other was caught by W.A. Wise, a member of the canteen staff, who thrust it into his jumper. With no time left to save his kit and his money, Wise put on a lifebelt and managed to swim free of the battleship before it sank. On being picked up by a boat, his first concern was for the kitten, which was none the worse off for its dip, and eventually accompanied Wise home to Ilford in Essex. The kitten was given the name 'Teddy', after the ship, though it never returned to sea after its adventures.

Norah was just one of many seadogs that served during the Great War. Peggy was the canine mascot of HMS *Iron Duke*, a dreadnought class battleship, and her presence was a considerable boost to morale for those on board, as these vignettes testify. Loaned by her owner for the duration of the war, Peggy soon became a favourite of the crew. Jumbo, another bulldog on board HMS *Iron Duke*, had been presented to Admiral Jellicoe by the actor Arthur Playfair, and was an inseparable companion of Peggy's. Peter Shaw Barker in his 1933 book *Animal War Heroes* relates that Jumbo was very protective of Peggy when other dogs were about, and that 'he once attacked an Airdale belonging to Admiral Burney and chased it into the stern sheets of a picket boat where a fierce fight ensued. They were only separated with the help of sailors with mops.' In due course, Peggy and Jumbo had a litter of five bulldog pups together. Peggy's sense of mischief was evident in her great enjoyment at carrying off any loose items left on deck, and stashing them away in her kennel. She was an enthusiastic participant in the ship's football team, whether on deck or on shore, and was not above invading the pitch when egged-on by spectators who were dissatisfied by the team's performance. In accordance with the agreed arrangement, Peggy returned to her owner in 1919 once the war was over. A portrait of Peggy was painted to sell in order to raise funds for St Bartholomew's Hospital, a charitable cause she had personally supported before, when collecting at Harrods department store, accompanied by a nurse. In January 1920, it was decided that Peggy herself should be included in an auction sale to raise money for Barts, and so she became 'Lot 21', raising sixty guineas for the charity. The purchaser of Peggy generously presented her back to the delighted crew of HMS *Iron Duke*, by now based with the Mediterranean Fleet, who sent a destroyer to collect her, a privilege afforded to few dogs. Peggy spent the last two and half years of her life happily in the care of A. B Viney on board HMS *Iron Duke*, for which he received a certain sum for her keep. She would sleep alongside Viney, with him using her as a pillow. When Peggy died after a short illness in June 1923, she was given a sailor's burial, and lowered over the side of the ship.

Old Bill, a wired-haired terrier, became the mascot of HMS *Falmouth* in rather unusual circumstances. In early August 1914, shortly after the outbreak of war, HMS *Falmouth* came across a fleet of five German fishing trawlers whilst on patrol in the North Sea. Acting on orders to take as prisoners any enemy crew, and to sink their vessels, four of the five ships were duly dispatched, with one old wooden boat left. After trying ineffectually to sink her with three rounds of shellfire, a boarding party attempted to blow her up using TNT. Though parts of the ship were thrown sky-high, the main body of the ship remained, and the decision was made to ram her, to prevent the derelict vessel being a hazard to shipping. After a few attempts, the ship was split clean in two, and to everyone's surprise a terrier appeared on one of the still floating halves. Bruised and barking furiously, the dog was remarkably unscathed after the encounter, and a boat was immediately sent from HMS *Falmouth* to rescue him. The dog was wearing a chain collar and brass name plate, inscribed with his name 'Fritz', so in spite of being abandoned to his fate on the trawler, he must have originally had an owner who cared enough to give him his own engraved collar. Adopted as the mascot of HMS *Falmouth*, he was patriotically re-christened with 'Old Bill', no doubt in homage to the comic creation of the same name by Bruce Bairnsfather. Old Bill was on board the *Falmouth* for the sinking of the German cruiser *Mainz*, and was even wounded three times during the Battle of Jutland. The *Falmouth* was sunk in August 1916 by torpedoes, after a sustained attack from Zeppelins L11 and L31 and two U-boats. Old Bill was rescued along with the crew, and went to live at Plymouth Barracks, where he remained a popular pet, living to a ripe old age and eventually dying of natural causes.

As the experience of Old Bill relates, the sea sometimes presented unexpected opportunities for crews to add to their number of pets. When some unusual circumstances found the crew of HMS *Glasgow* in possession of a magnificent pig, it was enthusiastically adopted as the ship's mascot. The pig originally hailed from SMS *Dresden*, a German light cruiser, where it had most likely been kept aboard as a source of fresh meat. Following a successful encounter for the British at the Battle of the Falkland Islands in December 1914, HMS *Glasgow* gave chase to the fleeing SMS *Dresden*. The Germans responded by scuttling the ship off the coast of Chile on 15 March 1915, leaving the unfortunate pig on board. Managing to swim clear of the sinking *Dresden*, the pig made for the nearby Royal Navy ships, and was rescued from the sea (after a considerable struggle) by a petty officer. The pig was dubbed 'Tirpitz', despite being female, after the German Admiral Alfred von Tirpitz, and jokingly awarded an Iron Cross for staying with the *Dresden* after the crew had abandoned ship. The pig became a favourite pet of the crew, as this affectionate photograph suggests. This wasn't the end of the adventures of Tirpitz the pig, however. After a spell at the Royal Navy training facility on Whale Island in Portsmouth harbour, she was later auctioned to raise funds for the British Red Cross, fetching 400 guineas (approximately £20,000 in todays' money). The details of her subsequent years are unknown, but we do know that in 1919, her then owner William Cavendish-Bentinck, 6th Duke of Portland, had her head stuffed, mounted and gifted to the Imperial War Museum in London. Her trotters were made into a carving knife and fork, and were used on the subsequent HMS *Glasgow*, before finding a home with Tirpitz's head in the Imperial War Museum.

The illustrated periodical *The Sphere* ran a spread on maritime animal life in March 1917 entitled 'Day by Day in the Royal Navy', featuring by several photographs, including a cat sitting on top of a 12-inch gun on board an unspecified ship, and two little Sealyhams posing with a sailor on deck. In the accompanying article celebrating the Noah's ark of mascots and companions at sea, *The Sphere* observed:

> Every ship has its pet, sometimes cats, sometimes dogs, and sometimes a monkey or other animal acquired under some special circumstances, which gives the pet his place of peculiar privilege on board. Cats are great favourites because of the homely feeling they give to a ship. Their coolness under fire is often remarkable.

For some, cats on board brought not just companionship and homeliness, but good luck. The society publication *The Tatler* celebrated the successful British raid on the Belgian port of Bruges-Zeebrugge in April 1918 with the picture of Vice-Admiral Alfred Carpenter and Commander Osborne of HMS *Vindictive* holding the ship's mascots, two black cats. *The Tatler* opined, 'Never, we suppose, has a ship had as great a need of mascots plus brave men as "Vindictive" had when she went under heavy fire and lay alongside the Zeebrugge Mole…' A month after this picture was published, HMS *Vindictive* was sunk on purpose as a 'blockship' after running aground at the Second Ostend Raid on 10 May 1918. What became of the cats is not known.

Ships' mascots could hinder as well as help in combat, as one ship's dog discovered when it fell overboard during a destroyer attack intended to flush out zeppelins. In the midst of the attack, permission was requested to lower a dinghy to pick up the dog, which was duly granted, and the dog rescued. Illustrator D. Macpherson recreated the scene for *The Sphere* in 1917, with his informant musing:

> *Lord knows what the Hun made of it. He was rumbling round and dropping bombs, and the dinghy was digging about for all she was worth, and the dog fiend was swimming for Dunkirk. It must have looked rather mad from above. But they saved the dog fiend, and then everybody swore he was a German spy in disguise.*

Though at first perhaps surprising, true sea creatures such as sea lions were affected by the war, and were pressed into service to contribute to the war effort. The call to arms meant many men left their chosen professions for the front lines, which had implications for the creatures under their care. *The Illustrated Sporting and Dramatic News* ran a photographic feature showing zoo-keepers from the Zoological Gardens in London saying goodbye to their charges in the early months of the war. Pictured is Mr G.W Graves, one of more than thirty London Zoo employees who responded to the call to enlist, bidding farewell to one of the sea lions in his care. According to his staff card in the Zoological Society of London archives, Graves survived the war, and returned to work at the Zoo.

A remarkable naval experiment involving sea lions came to light after the war was over, deemed so unlikely that when *The Illustrated London News* first heard of it, they believed it to be a hoax. The suggestion that attempts were made to train sea lions to hunt submarines did seem far-fetched. However, after a thorough investigation, they were satisfied enough with its authenticity to publish a lavish spread on it in April 1919:

> In the summer of 1917 the Admiralty hit on a novel way of hunting submarines. It was simply to employ tame sea-lions (Otaria Gillespie) to track them down-the idea being that the sea-lion could be taught to distinguish the noise of a submarine's propeller and to follow it in the hope of getting food. A buoy would be attached to the animal, and a trawler would follow the buoy and drop a depth charge when the sea-lion appeared to have found the submarine.

Wearing wire muzzles to prevent them from going on unsanctioned fishing expeditions, the sea lions would be released when a U-boat was suspected to be in the vicinity, and to this end, two Californian sea lions, a male named Billy and a female named Queenie, were put into training. Initial tests were carried out in a lake, before moving to Portsmouth harbour to work with real submarines. Problems with the system included the sea lions being distracted by other passing noises, such as other ship's propellers, and issues with the visibility and durability of the floats around the sea lions' necks. Large floats placed too great a strain on their necks, whilst small floats were difficult to see. The gut line connecting the float to the sea lions often broke, with thick wire proving an unsatisfactory substitute. It was also realised that when the weather was warm, the sea lions' behaviour was found to be somewhat lacking.

A more successful deployment of creatures at sea was the use of white mice as fume detectors on board Royal Navy submarines, to warn of the presence of petrol and other fumes. Though not deployed at sea, slugs were discovered to have a similar capacity for detecting mustard gas, thanks to the research of the American mollusc expert, Dr Paul Bartsch. When he discovered slugs had got into the furnace room of his home, he observed them recoil and become visibly distressed by the fumes. Further tests showed slugs to be sensitive to even low concentrations of gas, making them a useful (and low maintenance) early warning system for stealth gas attacks.

From the miniature to the mighty, the war impacted even on the lives of enormous sea creatures, such as whales. Two aerial images, published after the war in 1919 in *The Illustrated*

London News, show how, from the air, the silhouette of a whale could easily be mistaken for a submarine beneath the surface of the water. *The Illustrated London News* reported that a policy of 'when in doubt, bomb' was adopted, making whales an unwitting casualty of the war.

Though some whales were mistaken for U-boats when viewed from the air, in death, a floating whale could similarly be mistaken for a downed zeppelin. The throat and abdomen of the whale becomes distended with the gases of decomposition, causing it to be buoyed upwards in the water, belly first. On 17 October 1914, the lifeboat team at Margate set out to rescue possible survivors of a 'sinking zeppelin' that had been spotted out at sea. They returned disappointed, as the zeppelin was discovered to be merely a bloated whale carcass, floating in the water. Eager crowds gathered to see the prisoners of war they imagined to be plucked from the stranded zeppelin, but they too were disappointed. Instead, further down the coast at Birchington, the 61ft long body of a female common rorqual whale was later washed up on to the beach, probably the victim of a mine, rather than an aerial attack. William Plane Pycraft, the eminent zoologist and regular contributor to *The Illustrated London News*, was there in his official role as an employee of the Natural History Museum, and set about the slippery business of taking the whale's measurements at low tide. The two white lines in the photograph later in this chapter mark the size of the wound on the whale's body; Pycraft reports that the enormous gash in the abdomen could easily have accommodated a large armchair, with more room besides. The war had started only months before, but already the potential impact even on sea life could be seen. Though it was just one death in a war in which millions would die, there seems a terrible waste of life and a deal of pathos in the loss of a creature as majestic as the Birchington whale.

Though bombs and mines were bad news for the whales, their corpses could contribute to the war effort. In 1913, in response to a mass stranding of fifty sperm whales in Cornwall, the Natural History Museum was given the rights to collect whales and other cetaceans washed up on our shores; until then, a 1324 statute had only granted this to the Crown, the creatures being known as 'Fishes Royal'. The data gathered provided useful information when little was known about these rarely seen mammals. Pycraft highlighted the opportunity of using beached whales, porpoises and dolphins as an under-utilised source of protein when meat was rationed. He even went to the lengths of sampling some, when a very elderly, deceased whale, measuring 11ft and weighing nearly half a ton, came under his care. He also reproduced menus in his regular editorial column in *The Illustrated London News* from a whale steak luncheon given at the American Museum of Natural History on 8 February 1918, in the interests of food conservation. Pycraft relates that the whale liver was tough, though similar to bullock's liver in flavour, with every promise of it making a good soup. The flesh from the blade bone was rubbery, and the meat from other parts of the whale varied in tenderness, rather than flavour. Whale oil was also used to prevent trench foot when rubbed into the foot to form a waterproof barrier, and could also be used in explosives.

The First World War touched the lives of a wide range of creatures at sea, from the tiny white mouse, to the mighty whale. The presence of mascots and pets on board, and the lengths that men would go to protect and care for them reflects a basic need for companionship and affection in the midst of total war. Human creativity and resourcefulness can be seen through the perhaps unexpected roles that animals fulfilled at sea, from submarine hunting sea lions, to fume detecting mice. From pigs to parrots, from monkeys to mice, these creatures played their part at sea in the greatest conflict the world had ever experienced.

The magnificent pig, Tirpitz, mascot of HMS *Glasgow*, pictured in *The Graphic* in April 1916.

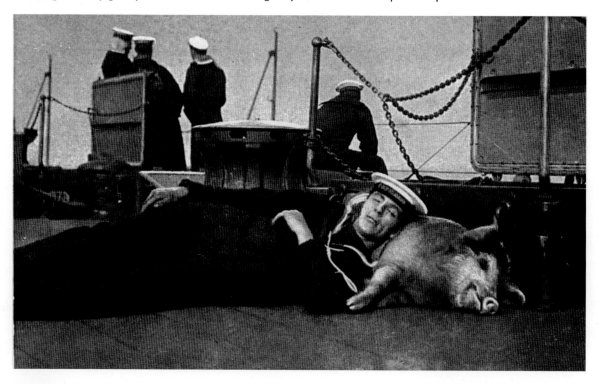

A ship's dog being rescued after falling overboard during a destroyer attack in 1917.

The keeper of the sea lions at London Zoo bidding farewell to one of his charges before going to war.

Billy, a Californian sea lion, being fed through a trap door in his muzzle.

SEA-LIONS THAT HUNTED U-BOATS: A REMARKABLE NAVAL EXPERIMENT.

AN AQUATIC ANIMAL TRAINED IN U-BOAT HUNTING: A SEA-LION
CLIMBING UP THE SHELL-BACK OF A SUBMARINE.

AT REST ON THE DECK OF A SUBMARINE WHICH IT HAS TRACKED:
A SEA-LION BEING TRAINED BY THE NAVY.

Part of a news feature from The Illustrated London News featuring 'Sea Lions that Hunted U-Boats: A Remarkable Naval Experiment'.

An aquatic animal trained in U-boat hunting: a sea lion climbing up the shell-back of a submarine.

At rest on the deck of a submarine which it has tracked: a sea lion being trained by the Navy.

White mice as fume detectors: an officer of the Royal Navy giving the mice an airing on deck.

Felines and fire power: a ship's cat provides a striking contrast to the enormous 12-inch gun on which it sits aboard an unspecified ship.

Two little Sealyham terriers posing with a sailor on deck.

Vice-Admiral Alfred Carpenter (right) and Commander Osborne (left) of HMS *Vindictive* with the ship's mascots, two black cats.

THE WAR IN THE AIR EXHIBITION: WHALES MISTAKEN FOR SUBMARINES.

FROM THE R.A.F. EXHIBITION OF COLOURED PHOTOGRAPHS AT THE GRAFTON GALLERIES.

A WHALE SWIMMING UNDER WATER PHOTOGRAPHED FROM THE AIR: SHOWING THE RESEMBLANCE TO A SUBMARINE WHICH CAUSED MANY TO BE BOMBED.

A "NEUTRAL" OF THE SEAS OFTEN MISTAKEN FOR A U-BOAT: AN AIR PHOTOGRAPH OF A LARGE WHALE SPOTTED FROM A BRITISH AIR-SHIP.

A page from *The Illustrated London News* showing how, from the air, a whale could be mistaken for a submarine.

A whale washed up at Birchington in Kent, likely killed by a mine.

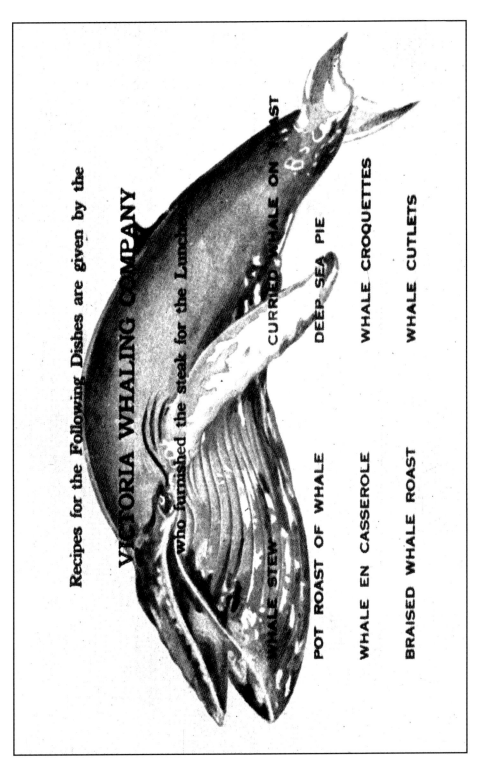

Whale meat-based dishes as a potential supplement to rations as suggested at a whale steak luncheon, given at the American Museum of Natural History in February, 1918.

Peggy the bulldog mascot of HMS
Iron Duke.

Old Bill the wired-haired
terrier mascot of HMS
Falmouth.

Chapter 2
The dogs of war

The Sphere, looking back after the end of the war in March 1919, reflected:

Dogs have helped substantially in the winning of the war – mascots, sentinels, dispatch carriers, Red Cross dogs, all have taken their part, and played it bravely to the finish. They were the sentinels, watchful at their posts and never sleeping, quicker than any human to give warning of a movement of the enemy, and the dogs of the Red Cross, who sought the wounded and brought back a scrap of uniform to say that they had found someone who needed more help than they could give. There were dogs who, masked like the horses and men, went forward through clouds of poison gas and dense fire with despatches and messages across ground where no man could live. They won through and brought their despatches or they died on the way, for nothing less than death could stop them, and very often they arrived with their messages wounded and injured, but with the despatches safe.

The considerable canine contribution to communications and surveillance during the war was largely due to the vision of dog training pioneer Lieutenant-Colonel Edwin Hautenville Richardson. Richardson was convinced of the potential of dogs to work as sentries, patrols and messengers on the front lines, and following the success of early experiments, the British War Office requested he established a British War Dog School, which he duly did in 1917 at Shoeburyness in Essex. Using gentle ways and encouragement rather than punishment for undesirable behaviour, the dogs were trained to overcome obstacles such as fences and streams, and to be able to dash fearlessly through a line of attacking infantry or clouds of smoke and gas. The dogs were able to traverse difficult and shell-scarred terrain with great speed and ease, making them highly desirable as messengers. At the start of the war, there were no military dogs in the British Army, save a solitary Airdale terrier who served as a sentry with the 2nd Battalion Norfolk Regiment, before being killed by a shell on the Aisne in France. So successful was Richardson's scheme that, in due course, there was a shortage of suitable dogs and appeals were made to members of the public to give their dogs to the war effort, on the assurance that they would be well fed and looked after (an attractive option for some, at a time of food scarcity.) Battersea Dogs Home in London (then known as Home for Lost Dogs at Battersea) was used as a source of canine recruits, with the search for dogs being rolled out to dogs' homes in Manchester, Birmingham, Liverpool and Bristol. The police were encouraged to round up stray dogs for this cause as well. Not every dog was suitable for this kind of work; certain breeds were seen as preferable, such as sheep dogs, collies, lurchers, Irish terriers, Welsh terriers, deerhounds and Airdales. Curiously, Richardson believed that any dog with a 'gaily carried tail, which curled over its back or sideways' was rarely of use to the school, and breeds such as retrievers (too compliant and lacking in independence of thought) and fox terriers (too fond of play) were also not favoured.

Dogs could also be trained to seek out the injured on the battlefield, and alert ambulance crews as to their location. Artist Eduardo Matania (father of Fortunino Matania) elegantly depicted a wounded French soldier at the Marne being discovered by a regimental dog. The piece was accompanied by a description of the event, given by a correspondent who had interviewed the wounded man:

> He was wounded by a piece of shell in the arm, by a bullet in the jaw, and a sword cut on the head, and lay on the battlefield half covered by the bodies of his dead comrades. Suddenly he felt caresses on his face. It was the regimental dog, which had been trained to carry back to the encampment the képis [cap] of wounded men. In this case the dog hesitated. 'Go and inform my mates,' urged the soldier. The dog understood and trotted off, bringing back two ambulance bearers, who picked up the wounded man. The dog is an old hand at this work. He goes regularly into the firing line, and when the fire is intense he digs a hole and buries himself.

Sentry dogs were also employed on the Western Front. Their keen sense of hearing helped keep watch for enemy snipers, or patrols who may be wandering too near to their lines.

Whether as sentries, messengers or ambulance dogs, canines on the front lines required billeting. In October 1915 *The Illustrated London News* reproduced a photograph of a canine camp, showing the accommodation provided for French ambulance dogs in a terraced colony of dugouts.

Transport and pest control were two other ways in which dogs contributed to the war effort. Dogs, accustomed to pulling milk carts in Belgium, were tasked with transporting ammunition, supplies and even machine guns to the front lines. Dogs of the French canine corps wore a special saddle harness, coupled in pairs by a light, connecting bar to a little supply cart. Dogs also helped make daily life in the trenches more bearable by catching the rats that were legion.

Rats destroyed equipment by gnawing leather straps; their urine spread disease; they bit men, thieved food and disturbed sleep, making pest control a priority. Special dogs for ratting, such as terriers, were brought in, with a price offered per tail of every rat caught.

Dogs on the home front too were able to 'do their bit' by collecting charitable donations for the war effort. Though dogs had been used to rustle up financial support for charities since Victorian times, the outbreak of war brought with it a new zeal, with dogs, sometimes in costume or attached to a harness, being roped in to utilise their sentimental appeal. The sentimental appeal of dogs is allied with their ability to act as transport in one postcard depicting a French casualty of the war, who is using a dog to pull his wheeled chair, and selling images of himself and the dog as a means to pay for the dog's food.

As the wartime wool shortage worsened, some dogs were even able to contribute their hair. Under the auspices of the British Dog Wool Association, combings from long-haired breeds such as Pekingese, Chow, collie and Pomeranian were harvested, sorted, sterilised and carded. The dog wool was then hand spun into warm, lightweight yarn to make garments for the war effort, such as socks.

The companionship, loyalty and solace that dogs brought may have been given what seems to modern eyes as a sentimental portrayal in the press, but the therapeutic and morale-boosting effect of canine companionship could be a powerful force for good. Men who were in dangerous, highly stressful situations, as well as those who were convalescing, found release, comfort and diversion in the company of dogs. There are many touching photographs in the Mary Evans Picture Library depicting the effect a dog's companionship can have on morale: an image of an Austrian soldier pausing from the fight to caress a regimental dog in a bleak-looking trench in 1915; a heart-warming photograph of Leo the Great Dane belonging to the 2/6th Battalion of North Staffordshires photographed standing up on his hind legs giving a soldier an affectionate greeting. An illustration on a postcard entitled 'Pals' portrays a blinded veteran, wearing the blue serge uniform of a hospital patient, putting his arm round a friendly collie dog, and in 'Captured at Courcelette', a British soldier poses cheerfully with a French dog that has been liberated from the Germans in the Somme region of northern France. The uplifting power of dogs can be seen in one photograph from the home front. Colonel Hall Walker, the Master of the Cheshire Foxhounds, invited wounded soldiers from local hospitals to be entertained to lunch and attend the Cheshire Hunt Puppy Show in the summer of 1916, where they were photographed with some of the puppies. The canine cuddles received here can only have served to lift spirits, speed recovery and, arguably, may have helped mend the invisible mental wounds sustained in the trauma of conflict.

Animal welfare was a priority of charities such as the RSPCA and Blue Cross during and after the war. Officially, soldiers were not permitted to bring their pets with them on active service, though some did successfully smuggle their pets, or adopt creatures in their place of posting. For soldiers' dogs left behind, special provision was made by the RSPCA kennels, providing accommodation for 500 dogs at Hackbridge in Surrey. The RSPCA also organised a fund to help soldiers bring back their mascots and pets after the war was over, assisting with the quarantine fees and other expenses. Without this help, soldiers would have been forced to have their animals destroyed, or left to the mercy of strangers abroad. The risk of rabies from animals secretly smuggled into the country was high, with an earlier outbreak attributed to an unscreened dog being imported by airplane. For those soldiers whose dogs had to be left behind in Blighty, help was at hand in the form of the charming ladies of the Hippodrome theatre in London, who organised and ran a scheme to care for the dogs of soldiers. All members of the Hippodrome revue *Business as usual*, some sixteen actresses, posed with their adopted pets for a spread published in *The Sketch* in February 1915.

Whilst dogs were used to aid the war effort in many ways, excessive fondness for pets in wartime could have a detrimental effect. Society ladies lavishing their lap dogs with expensive treats at a time of national shortages was seen as a particular vice. One scathing sketch by George L. Stampas in *The Bystander* refers to a 1915 court case, which roused Mr Justice Avory to comment that such behaviour at a time when 'every shilling in the country was required for the purpose of preserving our very existence as a nation, it was rather shocking to hear of such sums as £500 being wasted on ladies' pets.'

Some dogs found themselves as unwitting witnesses to history. One sad, covert snap shows Prince Lichnowsky, German Ambassador to London, leaving the Embassy at Carlton House Terrace for the last time, accompanied by his wife Mechtilde and pet dachshund after war was declared. The ambassador had strived through diplomatic means to avert the impending war, but to no avail. In *Margot at War: Love and Betrayal in Downing Street, 1912-1916*, Anne de Courcy writes, 'She [Margot Asquith, the Prime Minister's wife] found the Ambassador's wife, the Princess, lying on a sofa, her dachshund beside her and her eyes red and swollen with weeping. The dachshund yapped at Margot and the Princess wept, pouring out her misery at events and concluding by expressing her dislike of the Kaiser.' Mechtilde, an Anglophile author and dog lover, went on to publish a book after the war called *On the Leash*, on her reflections on London life and of her beloved dachshund. As enemy aliens, the Lichnowskys had to return to Germany after war was declared, but the esteem in which they were held is reflected in the special train that was provided for their departure, and the guard of honour that was mounted for them at Harwich.

The Kaiser's love of dachshunds was well documented, reinforcing for some their negative Germanic associations. Two particularly bad-tempered dachshunds belonging to the German Emperor, named Wadl and Hexl, almost caused an international incident when they set upon the heir-presumptive Archduke Franz Ferdinand's priceless golden pheasant on a semi-official visit to his country seat, Château Konopiště. Though this was no doubt a distressing episode (not least for the pheasant), the Archduke would soon have bigger problems to face than the Kaiser's belligerent dachshunds: he would be assassinated at Sarajevo in June 1914, triggering the hostilities that would leading to the outbreak of the war. Even in exile at Huis Doorn in the Netherlands after the First World War, the Kaiser was accompanied by his faithful dachshunds, five of whom were buried in the surrounding parklands. One German postcard depicts a pensive Kaiser in exile, with an equally pensive-looking dachshund seated next to him on a bench.

When the Kaiser's German Shepherd 'Lux' was captured by the Allies near La Fontaine de la Sauveniere in 1918, the event was commemorated on a postcard.

Tales of daring dogs during the Great War remain engaging and surprising, even a century after their heroic acts took place. One rough-coated collie cross was responsible for saving the life of Able Bodied Seaman John Cowan, of HMS *Formidable*, which was torpedoed in January 1915, in stormy conditions off Portland in Devon. After the ship sunk, a pinnace or light boat was blown along the coast to Lyme Regis, where it was landed on the beach, not far from the Pilot Boat Hotel. Landlady Mrs Atkins offered her pub to help care for the men, with locals bringing blankets, food, cigarettes and hot water bottles. Mrs Atkins' dog, Lassie, realised that one of the men, Cowan, who had been brought in as dead was in fact still alive, and managed to revive him using her warmth, by licking and nuzzling him for half an hour. The miraculous saving of Cowan's life earned Lassie fame and a silver collar, which she reportedly did not like wearing. She is pictured here at Crufts, framed with a life belt. Lassie and Cowan shared the front page of the *Daily Mirror*, along with a picture of the Christmas truce on 8 January 1915. Lassie may be, in part, the canine inspiration behind the film star Lassie, the heroic dog who performed daring rescues against the odds.

Tales of other courageous and faithful dogs abound: Bruce, an Irish terrier, was the pet of Captain A. Noel Loxley of HMS *Formidable*, the same ship that Cowan hailed from. When the ship was torpedoed and began to sink, an eyewitness described how the faithful hound stayed on the bridge with his master to the last. Both master and dog went down with the ship; Bruce's body was later discovered washed up on Chesil Beach in Dorset. He was later buried at nearby Abbotsbury Gardens.

Mirza, faithful even after death, was a soldier's dog, who refused to leave her master's grave. *Le Petit Journal*, a French periodical with a taste for dramatic illustrations, reproduced a full page image portraying this event in 1916. One faithful dog defended its former home during the entry of the Germans into Vailly, a small town lying on the river Aisne in France. Despite the absence of his owners and the wreckage around it, the dog still howled and kept watch over the few pieces of remaining furniture.

Some mascots became well known while on active service, but others had a long-standing reputation before they joined the ranks. One such mascot was a dog called Scotty, who had been the pet of Captain Scott of the Antarctic, and even accompanied him on an expedition to the South Pole in 1912. Scotty also went with the relief party to search for his late master's body, and was the first to find him. Scotty was presented to the 3rd Battalion, City of London regiment as their mascot, and was pictured 'in uniform' with his custodian, to whom he was devoted. *The Tatler* reported in July 1915 that 'Scotty when he first joined the regiment was very fierce, and rumour says the sudden decease of three donkeys was put on his defaulter's sheet.'

Manfred von Richthofen, also known as the Red Baron, was a German flying ace with eighty hits officially credited to his name. There was great interest in the Red Baron, with his 1917 autobiography *Der Rote Kampfflieger* being translated into English by J. Ellis Barker and published in 1918, while the war was still raging. He is pictured with his beloved dog Moritz, whom he wrote with great affection, 'The most beautiful being in all creation is the genuine Danish hound, my little lap-dog, my Moritz.' Bought in Ostend in Belgium for five marks as a pup, Moritz the 'little lap-dog' grew to an enormous size, once even accompanying Richthofen as an 'observer' in his plane. Richthofen described how Moritz would share his bed, and also how the dog destroyed many a billiard ball and billiard cloth in his 'playing' of the game. After Richthofen's unexpected death in combat on 21 April 1918, Moritz was adopted by Lieutenant Alfred Gerstenberg, a pilot of Richthofen's squadron Jasta 11, and lived on Gerstenberg's farm into old age.

'Rin-Tin-Tin' was a brown Alsatian, who achieved worldwide fame as a dog film star in the 1920s and 30s. He started life behind German lines at Metz in northeast France in September 1918, where he was discovered by an American soldier, Lieutenant Lee Duncan, when the dog was thought to be just a few days old. Duncan adopted the puppy, along with one of its siblings, naming it Rin-Tin-Tin, and eventually took him home to Santa Monica, California. Peter Barker Shaw reports in his 1933 book *Animals War Heroes* that when Rin-Tin-Tin's daring leaps at police dog trials happened to be captured on film, the cinematic potential of Rin-Tin-Tin became clear, with a contract with Warner Bros soon being sealed.

'Crump', the Belgian Griffon terrier, was a dog with an endearing penchant for tobacco. When the Marquis of Granby spotted Crump sitting up on his hind legs with a pipe in his mouth outside a farm between Ypres and Bailleul, he promptly purchased the dog and presented it to General Edward Montagu-Stuart-Wortley. Crump was reported to understand both French and English, and the General even had his car fitted out with a little table for Crump to sit upon when they travelled together. Crump survived the war, and returned with the General to Christchurch in Hampshire, where he enjoyed accompanying his master on rabbit shoots and fishing trips. In an unfortunate echo of his name, which was a wartime term for bombardment and the sound it made, Crump sadly died after being run over by a motor car.

The Tatler featured one picture of war veteran and champion ratter Morty in December 1920, with the following enthusiastic caption:

'Morty', the property of Lieut.-Colonel W.A. Murray, R.F.A. He went to France in August '14, and remained there the whole war, being continuously in the front line. Wounded once, and badly gassed, he wears two wounded stripes on his collar. He killed 300 rats at Passchendaele, and finally marched into Cologne, tail up, at the head of his brigade. Now living, full of scars and honours, at Bembridge, Isle of Wight.

It's pleasing to note that war animal stories were still of interest in the press, even some time after the war had ended. Though many creatures initially were unacknowledged for their role and sacrifice in the war, a charming illustration drawn for *The Sphere* in March 1920 bucks the trend, showing war dogs, specially decorated for the occasion, forming a procession through the streets of Milan.

Major Richardson's messenger dogs running the gauntlet of rifle fire during their training.

Messenger dogs leaping clear of barbed wire entanglements.

A depiction by Eduardo Matania in 1914 of a regimental dog discovering a wounded French soldier.

A FRENCH SENTRY and his WAR DOG on DUTY.

DRAWN BY PAUL THIRIAT, SPECIAL ARTIST OF "THE SPHERE" IN FRANCE

"WHAT WAS THAT?"—AN OUTPOST ON DUTY IN FRANCE WITH A FRENCH WAR DOG

The French sentries are making good use of dogs to help them in the course of their duties. After being first used as Red Cross dogs they are taken by the sentries and outposts to help both in the trenches and to keep a sharp watch against surprise attacks. This employment of dogs is, of course, a great help to the French outposts as a man may, and often does, fail to hear movements some distance away whereas a dog would rarely miss becoming aware of such movement. Some hundreds of these trained dogs are already at the front

A French sentry dog accompanied by a soldier on the Western Front, 1915.

THE SPHERE

AN ILLUSTRATED NEWSPAPER FOR THE HOME With which is incorporated "BLACK & WHITE"

Volume LXVI. No. 863. {REGISTERED AT THE GENERAL / POST OFFICE AS A NEWSPAPER} London, August 5, 1916 Price Sixpence.

ON GUARD ON THE WESTERN FRONT—A FRENCH WAR DOG

This French war dog is on the watch for any enemy sniper or patrol who may be wandering too close to the French lines. These dogs are specially trained to do this kind of sentry work. They are strong, powerful beasts, and their sense of hearing extends much further than that of the human sentries

'On guard on the Western Front-a French war dog': as pictured on the front page of *The Sphere* in August 1916.

A French sergeant and dog both wearing gas protection.

A canine camp: a terraced colony of dug-outs for French ambulance dogs.

Dogs of the French canine corps wearing a special harness for transporting ammunition.

A dog pulling a miniature Red Cross truck to collect charitable donations.

Laddie the long-haired dog collecting charitable donations, near Charing Cross railway station, London.

A dog pulling the wheelchair of a wounded French soldier.

An Austrian soldier stroking a regimental dog in a bleak-looking trench.

Leo the Great Dane belonging to the 2/6 North Staffordshires giving a soldier an affectionate greeting.

A blind veteran being comforted by a collie dog.

'Captured at Courcelette' a British soldier with a French dog, liberated from the Germans in the Somme region of northern France, 1918.

Wounded soldiers attending
Cheshire Hunt Puppy Show.

A wounded soldier taking his injured dog to the
Blue Cross for treatment.

THE ILLUSTRATED LONDON NEWS

REGISTERED AS A NEWSPAPER FOR TRANSMISSION IN THE UNITED KINGDOM, AND TO CANADA AND NEWFOUNDLAND BY MAGAZINE POST.

No. 4001.— VOL. CXLVII.   SATURDAY, DECEMBER 25. 1915.   With Photogravure Supplement General Sir Douglas Haig.   SIXPENCE.

The Copyright of all the Editorial Matter, both Engravings and Letterpress, is Strictly Reserved in Great Britain, the Colonies, Europe, and the United States of America.

The Illustrated London News featured this full page photograph on the cover of their 1915 Christmas day issue, showing a French Red Cross dog with an injured paw being bandaged by a doctor.

Kennels and care at RSPCA Hackbridge for the pets that soldiers had to leave behind.

Actresses of the Hippodrome theatre, London posing with adopted pets for *The Sketch* in February 1915.

Spoilt lap dogs portrayed in this scathing sketch of 1915 as a drain on valuable wartime resources.

The German Ambassador to Britain leaving the Embassy for the last time with his wife and their dachshund.

The Kaiser pictured in exile with one of his dachshunds after the war.

The Kaiser's German Shepherd Lux captured by the Allies near La Fontaine de la Sauveniere in 1918 was seen as sufficiently of interest to be commemorated on this postcard.

Lassie the life-saving dog and Seaman John Cowan, whom she miraculously revived.

Lassie at Crufts framed with a life belt.

Captain Loxley and his loyal terrier Bruce, depicted on the deck of HMS *Formidable*. Both man and dog went down with the ship after it was torpedoed in the English Channel in the early hours of New Year's morning, 1915.

Loyal Mirza, staying at her late master's grave, is visited by a soldier bringing her food.

A depiction by Eduardo Matania in *The Sphere* in April 1915, showing a faithful dog guarding its absent owners' house during the entry of the Germans into Vailly.

A FAMOUS MASCOT
The Late Captain Scott's Dog Joins the Army.

SCOTTY

The regimental mascot of the 3rd Battalion, City of London Regiment

SCOTTY

With the commanding officer and adjutant

Photographs by Wynford Swinburne

SCOTTY

In uniform, with his custodian, to whom he is devotedly attached

A detail from a page in The Tatler, dated 7 July 1915, reporting on a celebrity mascot: Scotty, the dog of the late Captain Scott, Polar explorer, who had become the regimental mascot for the 3rd Battalion, City of London regiment.

Manfred von Richthofen, aka the Red Baron, with his crew and beloved dog, Moritz.

Rin-Tin-Tin the rescued wartime pup turned world-famous dog film star.

A 1928 film poster starring Rin-Tin-Tin in 'Rinty of the Desert'.

Crump, the tobacco-loving terrier belonging to General Edward Montagu-Stuart-Wortley.

Morty the rat-slaying terrier, who saw action in France and survived the war.

The Sphere in March 1919 reminisced about some memorable dogs of the Great War, featuring the three following images. 'An accomplished spaniel: Motor cycling presents no difficulties to Stunter, the mascot of the Tank Corps, for owing to his experience of tanks as a means of transport he can balance himself quite comfortably on the bars of a motorcycle.'

'The massive bulldog, Gibby, sitting at the entrance to a dug out beside the commanding officer, was the mascot of a Canadian regiment. Although he was badly gassed on more than one occasion, he still continued to go into action with his men.'

'This dog went into the trenches with his master and afterwards accompanied the battalion when it went into billets behind the line. He is mutely enduring the ordeal of a bath in a small basin.'

A post-war procession in Milan celebrating war dogs, specially decorated for the occasion, depicted in *The Sphere* in 1920. The caption beneath the original image relates how "All the streets through which they[the dogs] were to pass became thronged with spectators, who came with biscuits, sweets, badges, flowers, and tri-colour flags to present to the heroes of the day…All the dogs - long-haired or short-haired, lop-eared or prick-eared, were covered with flowers, and each and all met with a tumultuous welcome."

Chapter 3
Birds in battle

The role of carrier pigeons in transmitting information during the First World War was invaluable. The homing instinct of these birds enabled messages to be sent via a small tube attached to the pigeon's foot, as can be seen in this picture of an American soldier of the Signal Corps in 1918, who is in the process of attaching a message. These were not the only birds who served or were affected by the war, however: canaries, chickens, swallows, swans and storks to name but a few who also found themselves caught up in the conflict. Whether as messengers, mascots, meat or music makers, birds lifted the spirits and saved lives, as these vignettes and archive images testify.

Where field telephones were inaccessible or unreliable, such as inside tanks or on submarines and planes, these winged messengers of war were a lifeline to the outside world. *The Graphic* featured a sequence in June 1917 demonstrating the preparation and departure of a carrier pigeon. As with horses and dogs in the service of their country, special arrangements had to be made to house and care for carrier pigeons. *The Illustrated London News* featured a picture in October 1915 showing converted motorbuses which served as a loft for carrier pigeons of the French Army. There are also examples of Austrian soldiers transporting carrier pigeons by dog in special boxes in 1918. When gas warfare was introduced on the Western Front, it was not only the soldiers who needed protecting from its harmful effects. In a photograph from 1917, German soldiers are pictured locking their carrier pigeons away in gas proof boxes in their dugout. Carrier pigeons were no strangers to close confines: the image of the release of a pigeon from a porthole in a tank in the Somme region of France in August 1918 has almost biblical echoes of the release of a dove to find land in the Old Testament story of Noah's ark.

Domestic birds caught up in the conflict when their homes were swallowed up by the warzones had a very different experience of war. This is how *The Sphere* reflected on the fate of pet birds in wartime, here in March 1919:

> *Amid the ruins of the house these men rescued a bird-cage undamaged and the bird within unhurt. Birds in the destroyed or deserted houses did not always meet with such a happy fate. During the evacuation of a little village, not far from Noyon, a family were compelled to leave behind them their canary. With tears in their eyes they came to the officer in charge and asked him to do what he could for their pet. Visiting the house a day or so later to see after the bird, the officer found the cage knocked over, the door open, a few feathers and a little pink blood upon the woodwork. That was all.*

Upon rescue, some birds were adopted by soldiers as pets, with others befriending wild birds, including blackbirds, thrushes and magpies. There are also cases of larger birds associating with soldiers. W.P Pycraft wrote an article accompanying several pictures in *The Sphere* in January 1917, reporting how some nesting white storks had taken a special interest in the British planes stationed at Salonika, Macedonia, with a picture of a stork perched on one of the aircraft. *The Sphere* also ran this feature in the same issue about a British officer of the Salonika army and his captured eagle. The picture was accompanied with this caption:

> *This magnificent golden eagle belongs to an officer on the Balkan front, and is so tame that strangers can handle him. When first caught he was only just fledged, a mere ball of fluffy feathers, but he flourished exceedingly in captivity and does full credit to his upbringing. He takes long flights daily, but never fails to return to his master, with who he is here seen indulging in a friendly tussle.*

Though compassion and companionship was offered by some to birds on the front lines, for others, the hunting of birds offered entertainment, sport and the opportunity to supplement their rations with fowl. One drawing by Frank Dadd, from *The Graphic* in February 1917, depicts young officers, not far from the front line in France, hunting partridge on horseback. *The Graphic* reports that, 'By persistently following them it was found possible to reduce them to an exhausted condition, and to knock a few on the head. The bags were small, but there was plenty of amusement and excitement in this novel form of sport.' On the home front, *The Tatler* ran two images as their front-page story on 10 November 1915, showing wounded Anzac and British troops enjoying a day's pheasant hunting: here hunting is portrayed as a therapeutic leisure activity (though not for the birds.)

In addition to keeping birds as pets and mascots, poultry-keeping was a way of supplementing diets and incomes through the production of eggs. Karswood Poultry Spice published a promotional book in 1919 entitled *Fortunes from Eggs*, with a view to encouraging discharged soldiers, amongst others, of the merits of poultry-keeping as a source of income. The archive holds images of chicken runs on the Western Front and in Gallipoli respectively, providing soldiers with fresh eggs. On the home front too, the birds were valued for their role in fleshing out food rations and, as in the trenches, underutilised space was converted to aid the war effort. Lord's Cricket Ground in London was used as a goose farm, the birds' close cropping of the turf helping to keep the grounds in check.

Geese on the Western Front found themselves in a more traditional role at Christmas, as a festive source of food. The taste of a cooked goose, and even the act of Christmas shopping, albeit in a war zone, must have brought a welcome evocation of home and Christmases past. The hearty festive fare, in the form of a Christmas goose, would have provided a boost to morale as well as nutrition of soldiers in the front line, whether it was their first Christmas of the war far from home, or their third. The enormous cheer and anticipation that a goose feast could bring is summed up in the jubilation of one particular drawing by Leslie Hunter, showing the return of the men to the trenches with their Christmas geese, after having purchased them from local towns and markets. On 30 December 1914 *The Illustrated War News* published a picture showing a group of soldiers cooking their geese out in the open on an improvised 'spit', constructed from rifles, a spade and sticks, along with the caption:

> There was no Christmas truce at the front. The grim realities of the war over-rode all considerations of sentiment, and the hope which was, for a while, common to both sides had to be left unfulfilled. None the less, the season was not without its little luxuries, and, thanks to the excellent work of the Army Service Corps and the thoughtfulness of sympathetic friends at home, there was no dearth of substantial necessities and comforts, as well as tobacco and cigarettes galore.

The news of the Christmas truce was not reported until early January, though it's interesting to note that a truce, which had been suggested by the newly appointed Pope Benedict XV, had been anticipated in the press. The caption relates that the soldiers were not in least put out by 'spasmodic artillery duels, and local fusillades' as they cooked. When Britain went to war just a few months before this picture was taken, it was widely believed that the war would be over by Christmas. There's no suggestion of ennui yet with the on-going conflict in these cheering pictures.

As well as serving as supplies, geese were sometimes adopted as regimental mascots. When A Battery of the 52nd Brigade Royal Field Artillery bought two geese in December 1915, their intention was to fatten them up to provide a good Christmas dinner for the officers' mess. However, someone in the Battery took a fancy to them and, after a mock trial to establish their fate, they were adopted as the official mascots of the Battery. Named Jimmy and Jane, they remained with the Battery until the end of the war. On being demobilised in 1919, there was some debate as to whether the geese should be quarantined at Dover. The troops decided to take matters into their own hands, and somehow smuggled the geese on board the train (no mean feat, as anyone who's ever had to grapple with a goose will know), only to be discovered by the landing officer. Eventually, the birds were allowed to travel, and spent a year at London Zoo, where they were admired by many visitors. In 1920, Jimmy died, and Jane went to live on a farm in Aston-Tirrold in Berkshire, where she lived with a number of other geese, with the run of several orchards, until her death in December 1931.

Geese could also serve as unofficial 'watchdogs', in the ancient tradition, when the geese of the Capitoline Hill in Rome warned of the invading Gauls, by raising the alarm. Geese were not the only winged watchdogs on the Western Front: *The Sphere* reported that a magpie had become the pet and guardian of a soldier's tent. Reportedly, no one dared touch anything the magpie protected, for fear of immediate attack by the bird.

An unnamed gunner, writing in *The Graphic* in February 1917 on wildlife on the battlefront, reported on how:

Magpies' nests are also to be found, although, as a rule, they prefer the long lines of poplar trees so common in Northern France. They stick tenaciously to one spot in nesting, and I have seen a pair, when their first nest was blown away with the treetop, calmly build another nest on the top of the shattered top of the standing stump. The shell had splintered the top of the stump into the shape a monstrous birch broom, and no doubt the magpies considered the whole affair arranged for their benefit.

The Illustrated London News published a drawing by artist Samuel Begg of migrating swallows in September 1915 as a striking full page. The simple sight and sounds of bird life in the most war-ravaged settings brought hope and lifted the viewer, even if only momentarily, above the carnage and chaos of the war, which had dragged on for over a year by the time this image was published. It is a reminder that other birds, beside the dove, can serve as a symbol of peace, and that nature's rhythm of the seasons and the migration of birds continues, almost oblivious, whilst humankind is engrossed with war.

Like the freedom of flight, the morale boosting effect of hearing birdsong, or a familiar tune, could be a tonic to soldiers. An illustration by Frederic de Haénén, drawn after official photographs, formed the front page of *The Illustrated London News* on 18 May 1918. Depicting the interior of a British hospital-train, the picture was entitled: *A song from home*, the caption noting that 'Everything is done to make the "wards" as bright and cheerful as possible, as in a hospital. Even canaries in cages may be hung near the cots on occasion to amuse patients with their song, recalling memories of home.'

In an essay in *The Graphic* in October 1916, J.H Leonard noted that, in spite of the combined factors of 'the vast amount of road traffic, the high explosives and the noise, the "gassing", the destruction of vegetation, the suspension of agricultural operations, and the warfare of the air', for nature it was 'business as usual', with some creatures on the front lines not only surviving, but thriving in the face of adversity. The essay was entitled *Nature's business as usual – how wildings survive in the war zone*, reflecting perhaps a surprising public interest in animal life on the front lines even while the war was still on. Included in the article was a photograph showing the swans of Ypres who had faced 'shot and shell' and 'lived through all the bombardments'. Three years into the war, 'animal interest' stories still featured in the press; the British appetite for stories about animals had not been dulled by the conflict.

Preparation and departure of a carrier pigeon, 1917.

GOING ! ————————————— British Official

————————————— GOING ! ————— Canadian Official

Canadian Official
GONE

A converted motor bus as a loft for carrier pigeons of the French Army.

Austrian soldiers with carrier pigeons transported by dog in 1918.

A carrier pigeon held tight before release from the belly of a tank in 1918.

German soldiers keeping carrier pigeons safe in gas proof boxes in 1917.

The fate of small birds in wartime : British soldiers pictured with a cage of rescued canaries in France; *The Sphere* reported these birds were the only survivors found among the ruins.

A British soldier poses with a cage of rescued canaries in France.

A soldier and a tame blackbird at the Marne, France.

A British soldier pictured with his pet thrush in 1916.

A Macedonian stork, who took great interest in the presence of the British RAF based in Salonika.

A British officer and
his pet golden eagle at
Salonika in 1917.

Young officers, by
the French front line,
hunting partridge on
horseback.

Wounded Anzac and British troops enjoying a day's pheasant hunting whilst convalescing in 1915.

FROM TRENCHES TO POULTRY PEN.

Average 263 Eggs per Bird in the Year.

A discharged Soldier thanks Karswood Spice for his brilliant success in egg-production.

30, Best Street, Old Hill,
near Dudley, Staffs.

To Karswood, Manchester.

Dear Sirs,—Enclosed you will find the result of 12 months' laying of my six White Leghorns, for the year finishing at October 7th, 1918. Totals for each bird (all trap-nested) :—No. 1, 289 ; No. 2, 225 ; No. 3, 266 ; No. 4, 272 ; No. 5, 251 ; No. 6, 275. Grand total—1,578 eggs in the complete year, an average of 263 eggs per bird.

I may mention I am a discharged soldier, and being unable to follow my employment I turned to poultry as the one means I knew something about of earning a living.

I had also to find a cheap method of feeding my birds without stinting them in the least, as I would have gone without myself to buy my fowls their food. My method I give you below, and I hope it will bring others to use Karswood Spice and meet the success they deserve.

I think you will agree with me my birds have done well, and in

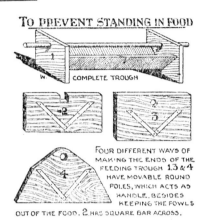

TO PREVENT STANDING IN FOOD

COMPLETE TROUGH

FOUR DIFFERENT WAYS OF MAKING THE ENDS OF THE FEEDING TROUGH 1,3 & 4 HAVE MOVABLE ROUND POLES, WHICH ACTS AS HANDLE, BESIDES KEEPING THE FOWLS OUT OF THE FOOD. 2 HAS SQUARE BAR ACROSS.

pre-War days I doubt if they would have done better. I knew my birds were good enough, but money was scarce, and I had to find the cheapest means of producing the eggs. It has been a great surprise to me, and I wish others to share in the good fortune I have had. I am specially, for that reason, asking you to publish my method, but, first, let me thank you, as a discharged Soldier, for bearing the entire cost (£178) of another outfit for Corporal Mason, the blind soldier, in the place of the one he lost in the sinking of the " Galway Castle."

My Method.

If the small poultry keeper will only try this method he will, at the cost of about 12/6, produce enough extra eggs to buy a £5 War Bond.

First go to your local Fish Dealer and arrange to take away the fishes heads and other fish offal which would otherwise go into the refuse bin. Then buy some Nut Kernel Meal, Maize Meal, and Middlings or Sharps. These three Meals, mixed together, I call " Mixed Meal," and in winter I use much more of the Maize Meal

A GOOD TYPE OF SOFT FOOD TROUGH

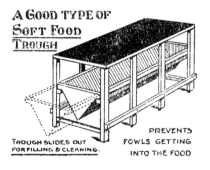

TROUGH SLIDES OUT FOR FILLING & CLEANING.

PREVENTS FOWLS GETTING INTO THE FOOD

The financial benefits of poultry keeping from the perspective an ex-service man writing in *Fortunes from Eggs*, a promotional book by Karswood Poultry Spice, published in 1919.

A sandbagged chicken coop and run, providing fresh eggs at Gallipoli.

British soldiers with a homemade hen house in a trench on the Western Front in France, circa 1916.

Lord's Cricket Ground converted into a goose farm, with the birds helping to crop the turf.

British soldiers buying their Christmas geese within earshot of the guns in France, 1916.

The cheerful return of soldiers with their Christmas geese to the trenches in 1914.

An improvised spit made from rifles, sticks and a spade to roast Christmas geese.

'The goose-step performed for the benefit of Mr Atkins by Christmas ducks': birds as entertainment.

'The Christmas goose that comes to Tommy's bugle call.'

A territorial magpie,
protecting his master's tent.

Swans that survived the
bombardment at Ypres.

The rhythm of nature and the migration of birds continues in spite of the war in Samuel Begg's striking drawing of swallows over the ruins of a destroyed town.

'A song from home', soldiers' spirits lifted by the joy of birdsong whilst onboard a hospital train in 1918.

Chapter 4
All creatures great and small

The Graphic featured a spread in November 1916 showing the diverse range of creatures adopted as mascots: 'The mascot is met with in many varieties on all our fronts, but nowhere in greater abundance than at the [London] Zoo, which has become a dumping-ground of regimental pets. Among them are half a dozen black bears from the Canadian Rockies, and a number of deer.'

Reflecting the nationality of their owners, bears were great favourites with Canadian troops as mascots. Just a few months after the war had begun, Canadian troops were already encamped on Salisbury Plain in England: a dominion of the British Empire, Canada was automatically enrolled when Great Britain declared war in August 1914. In November 1914, *The Illustrated Sporting and Dramatic News* reproduced a picture of Canadian troops on Salisbury Plain with a black

bear as their regimental pet. A bear mascot named Winnie, after Winnipeg in Canada, was smuggled to Britain by Lieutenant Harry Colebourn of The Fort Garry Horse, a Canadian cavalry regiment *en route* to the Western Front. The bear was left at London Zoo where she became very popular with visitors, including Christopher Robin Milne, son of the author A. A. Milne, who would go on to write his Winnie-the-Pooh stories based on his son's teddy bear, who was in part named after the animal.

Bears were not the only mascots to grace the Salisbury Plain-in the same issue of *The Illustrated Sporting and Dramatic News,* a member of A company of the 1st Battalion of Canadian troops posed with 'Tabby', a Persian cat that travelled across the Atlantic with them.

When America, previously pursuing a policy of neutrality and non-intervention, entered the war in 1917, their soldiers were accompanied by the usual array of animal mascots. Two soldiers of the American

Expeditionary Forces (known as 'Doughboys') were pictured in the same year, posing with their pet dachshund and a coati mundi (a type of raccoon).

'The British Army loves animals, and has adopted legions of them as pets and mascots, in addition to the horses and dogs enrolled officially.' So wrote *The Sphere* as part of a feature in March 1919 tellingly entitled 'Mascots of the British Army: their useful work during the war'. The air force also had their share of mascots, with rabbits and foxes counted amongst their number. An image survives of an RAF pilot with the fox mascot of his squadron, pictured circa 1916. If the original caption to this image is to be believed, the fox was allegedly fond of flying. Pilots of the Royal Flying Corps (the name of the army branch of the air force, before it merged with the Royal Naval Air Service to become the Royal Air Force) were photographed posing with their pet rabbits in front of their airplane in France circa 1918.

Larger animals such as goats were also kept as military mascots, some playing a more formal role, being entitled to ceremonial dress and other privileges as a full member of the battalion. Billy, the goat mascot of the Royal Welsh, was pictured in *The Sketch* at a football match in September 1914. His tunic bears the emblem of the regiment, the Prince of Wales' plumes. Less official was a stag who was kept as an unusual pet at a rest-camp in France, October 1916, and the young gazelle mascot adopted by a soldier in Mesopotamia, that featured in *The Graphic* in 1916.

Adopted creatures could reflect the local wildlife, leading to some rather unusual pets. Soldiers in warmer climes, particularly in the East, enthusiastically adopted chameleons, with their fly-catching abilities being especially prized. In January 1918, *The Illustrated Sporting and Dramatic News* reported on how chameleons had their names inscribed on their sides by their soldier-owners in indelible pencil, with a belt of thread round the chameleon's waist serving as a leash. Regiments held fly-catching competitions, with a cash prize for the winner's owner, providing much needed entertainment for the soldiers, as well as keeping down the fly population.

In a certain regiment, where practically every man possessed a chameleon, a fly-taking competition was held —100 piastres for the greatest number of flies eaten in five minutes, and 100 piastres for the longest drive…Towards the end of November the wild chameleons disappeared, and evidently hibernated; and one by one the tame specimens became gaunt and colourless and died, expect for a few whose owners kept them in boxes lined with cotton wool at night. Whatever his faults, and he is surely lacking in every desirable quality, the chameleon is an amusing creature, and has done much in this war to while away Thomas Atkins' dreary hours of heat and boredom, whilst his efforts to keep the fly pest in check have been most praiseworthy.

Other exotic animals such as camels and monkeys played their parts too. *The Illustrated Sporting and Dramatic News* in June 1916 depicted camels, but as transport rather than mascots, in a photograph of the advance of the specially created British Camel Corps (one of the four battalions of the Imperial Camel Corps Brigade) in the Sudan. An image of a camel foal, pictured with a British officer and born on active service, appeared as an exclusive picture in *The Sphere* in November 1918. Eduardo Matania in the same publication in September 1917 depicted the adventures of 'Bebe', the monkey mascot of an Italian officer. Bebe is shown returning triumphant with the Austrian flag he has just pinched from the enemy trenches, under a hail of bullets; he is given a hero's welcome by his delighted comrades. Also pictured is a sailor with a pet primate at Shotley Barracks in Suffolk, known as HMS *Ganges*, an on-shore training establishment for the Royal Navy. *The Graphic* published another spread entitled: *Our soldiers' love of animal pets: the use of mascots in the services*, featuring 'Billy' the baboon, of the South African heavy artillery, as well as 'Nancy', the springbok of the South African Scottish regiment.

Not all creatures were welcomed with such gusto. In *The Graphic* in February 1917, an unnamed gunner wrote:

> But perhaps the rats dominate everything. They are swarming in the trenches and dug-outs in appalling numbers. Night and day they hold high revel among one's belongings, and scamper wildly over one's face, in some cases stopping to take a nip en route. Rats will always leave a sinking ship, so perhaps that is the reason they find such happiness in our company, and, in spite of war's numerous alarms, refuse to leave us. Our superstitious ancestors, seeking for signs and portents, might have considered the presence of the rodents a certain omen of victory. It is extraordinary how the brutes increase. After a bad gas attack the trenches are full of dead mice, rats and beetles. One would expect a few days' peace and quiet. But no; in a few hours the beggars are just as numerous as ever. There must be an immense reserve army of rats waiting behind the front lines to take the place of the slain.

A plentiful supply of food, water and shelter in the trenches ensured a rat population explosion. The rats fed not only by scavenging for scraps from soldiers' discarded rations tins, but also from a more sinister and plentiful source: human flesh from the dead and dying out in no-man's land. With such an abundant supply of food, rats were reported to grow to the size of cats (a caption to one 1917 sketch in *The Illustrated London News* describes rats of 'aldermanic size'), and reproduced at an alarming rate, with 'swarms' of rats described in soldier's diaries and letters home. Attempts were made to control the population using rat catchers and terriers, with the incentive of a cash sum paid per tail. Ferrets were also in demand for ratting, causing their price in Ashford in Kent to rise from 1 shilling to 5 shillings in 1916. There were some creative responses to the rat problem, with rats treated as 'small game' and hunted as a trench sport. *The Illustrated London News* published a double page spread in April 1916, showing British soldiers in hot pursuit of a rat with a fixed bayonet, describing the scene as 'sport in self-defence'. Use of ammunition to hunt rats was discouraged on grounds of wastage. Despite the generally unwelcome presence of rats in the trenches, the press portrayed the problem as a cheery, everyday irritation in their reportage from the front. A cartoon-like cover of the French satirical magazine *La Baionnette*, dated May 1917, shows a British and a French soldier, holding an enormous fly and a rat; two great trench menaces. In one photograph, German soldiers pose cheerfully with the rats they have caught in the trenches: this image was considered fit to be made into a field postcard (a printed card with 'multiple choice' style answers to be deleted as appropriate, enabling quick communication that was approved by the censors).

Echoing the poultry farming initiative for ex-soldiers, a scheme for beekeeping as an occupation for those 'maimed' by the war was instigated by Lord Eglington, who set up a training school at Borland House, Kilmarnock. The demands of war meant that every possible resource had to be maximised in order to contribute to the war effort, and like Lord Eglington's bees, other creatures found themselves being deployed to meet new needs. With horses already in short supply, circus elephants in both Germany and Britain were requisitioned or borrowed for heavier war work, such as ploughing and transporting heavy loads. With circus workers away fighting the war, as many others were from a wide variety of occupations, and with restrictions on feed and travel, many travelling circuses were forced into dormancy for the duration of the war. 'Lizzie', a circus elephant turned munitions worker in Sheffield, was pictured in *The Illustrated War News* in February 1916. Previously of Sedgewick's travelling menagerie, Lizzie was 'taken on' by scrap merchant's Thomas Ward Ltd, where she worked hauling scrap metal, utilised to make munitions. *The Illustrated War News* reported that Lizzie could do the work of five horses and could draw eight tons easily.

The war impacted on animals' lives in ways that were difficult to predict. A severe potato shortage in Germany lead to the mass slaughter of pigs in 1915, known as Schweinmord, in an attempt by the German government to remove the perceived competition between people and pigs for potatoes. Nine million pigs were slaughtered, but the desired effect on the food shortage did not happen.

Another unforeseen casualty of the war was the rare European bison, *Bos bonasus*, also known as wisent. These were hunted to extinction in the wild by Germans occupying Poland, the last bastion of the bison in Europe. Previously under the protection of the Tsar, these endangered, forest-dwelling creatures were killed by German soldiers for both food and sport during 1915. Standing at over 6ft in height at the withers, these prehistoric beasts were larger than their descendants the American bison (also known as buffalo) with longer horns, and a yak-like abundance of hair at the head, neck and forelimbs. W.P Pycraft wrote passionately about the massacre of the bison in his weekly column in *The Illustrated London News*, which also published an accompanying illustration of a herd of bison in the ancient Białowieża Forest, scattering from the blast of a shell.

With the flight of civilians from their homes as the war encroached further into their lives, both farm and domestic animals were often left behind to fend for themselves in their owners' rush to escape. Soldiers' diaries report ravenous dogs roaming abandoned villages, and dairy cows with swollen udders wandering free, with nobody to milk them. In one photograph, a cow forms part of the civilian exodus and has literally been roped into pulling a refugees' cart from Ypres, Belgium in November 1914.

One cat became a mascot of a big-gun crew on the Western Front. *The Sphere* noted when it reproduced this picture in March 1919 that: 'Cats have proved themselves very useful during the war, and numbers of them have been under fire, both ashore and afloat. In the trenches they rendered inestimable service in the war against hordes of rats infesting them, and were popular pets with the men.' When Lieutenant Lekeux of the 3rd Artillery Regiment adopted a tiny kitten whilst on duty in the front line at Oud Stuivekenskerke, Belgium, little did he know that it would go on to save his life. White and fluffy with grey patches, the kitten was part of a litter of eight, discovered mewing piteously in a dugout one afternoon. Colleagues informed Lekeux that the kitten's mother had been killed that morning by enemy fire, and the kittens, still with their eyes closed, were now in danger of death as well. Lekeux took the kittens into his care but, despite his best efforts and a laborious programme of feeding them individually using a straw and milk, after two days only the white kitten was left alive.

The kitten was named 'Pitoutchi', as the closest approximation to the sound of a cat sneezing, after it caught a cold and sneezed frequently. The cat became a devoted friend of Lekeux, accompanying him on his duties in the trenches, and riding on Lekeux's shoulder when the ground became wet or muddy. Having missed the nursing of his own mother, Pitoutchi's growth was stunted, not exceeding 12in from nose tip to tail once fully grown. Though small, Pitoutchi was intelligent, and it was his quick wits that saved his master's life on a mission into no-man's land. Lekeux set out under cover of darkness to investigate suspicious enemy activity close to the front line. Pitoutchi accompanied him, on his usual spot on his shoulder. Realising that the Germans were digging a new line of trench, Lekeux crept off into a shell hole a few yards away to sketch the scene. Engrossed in his work, he didn't see three German soldiers crawling towards him on their bellies, with bayonets fixed; having seen his entry into the shell hole, they had come to investigate. Pitoutchi sprang to his master's aid by jumping out of the shell hole, causing the German soldiers to fire two shots, and the cat to tumble back into the hole unharmed. The Germans thought they'd mistaken a man for a small white cat, and laughed heartily; Lekeux and his cat escaped back to their trenches unscathed. Lekeux submitted a recommendation that the cat be decorated for saving his life, but sadly this never came to pass; even while the report was being considered, Pitoutchi disappeared. The cat had gone missing whilst Lekeux attended a parade that it was impossible to bring Pitoutchi along to; on his return, the cat had gone, either killed, or taken away by someone. Sadly, Lekeux never saw his cat again.

From bears to baboons, from bison to bees, to cats, cows, chameleons and even coati mundi, archival images offer a snap shot of the wide range of creatures from all over the world who found themselves involved with the conflict, and gives a taste of their many roles and differing experiences of war.

Bears at London Zoo, previously regimental mascots, respond to soldiers beckoning from above their enclosures.

Canadian troops and their regimental pet: a
black bear cub.

Tabby the Persian cat of A
company of the 1st Battalion
of Canadian troops, pictured in
November 1914.

Two American soldiers with their pets: a dachshund and a coati mundi.

On active service: a fox as a mascot, pictured in a harness.

An British pilot with the fox mascot of his squadron, pictured circa 1916.

British pilots with their pet rabbits, France 1918.

A handsome billy goat, the pet mascot of the Royal Welsh pictured at a football match in September 1914.

A stag as an unusual pet at a rest-camp in France, October 1916.

A soldier feeds his young gazelle mascot in Mesopotamia.

Billy the baboon, of the South African heavy artillery.

Nancy, the springbok of the South African Scottish.

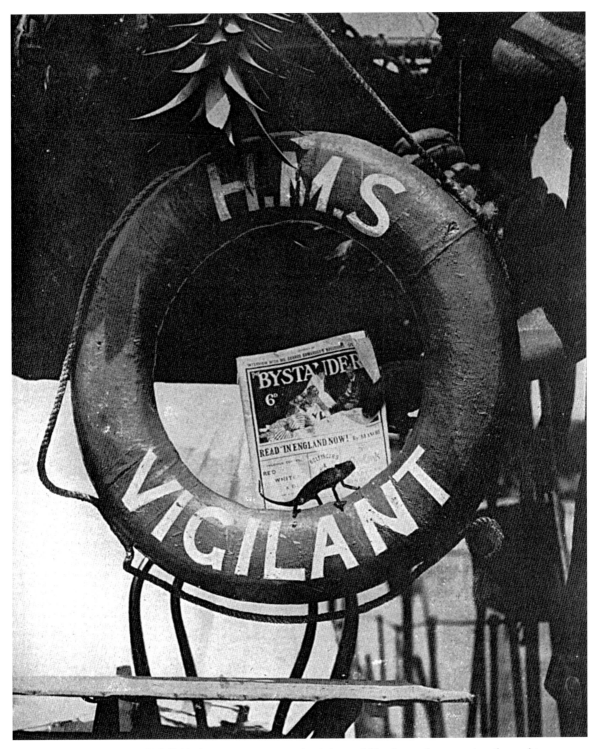

The chameleon mascot of HMS *Vigilant* poses against a backdrop of *The Bystander* magazine, framed in a lifebelt.

British Camel Corps in the Sudan, portrayed in *The Illustrated Sporting and Dramatic News* in June 1916.

This camel foal, pictured with a British officer, was born on active service, and appeared as an exclusive picture in *The Sphere* in November 1918.

Monkey business in the trenches: a depiction by Eduardo Matania in *The Sphere* in September 1917 of the adventures of Bebe, the monkey mascot of an Italian officer.

A sailor with a monkey mascot at Shotley Barracks in Suffolk.

An illustration from 1917 showing rats that were reportedly the size of cats.

An undated picture of a French rat catcher, festooned with his kill.

An official French rat catcher with his terrier and a display of dead rats.

British soldiers in hot pursuit of a rat with a fixed bayonet.

The front cover of the French periodical *La Baionnette*, dated May 1917, showing a British and a French soldier, holding an enormous fly and a rat: two great trench menaces.

German soldiers pose cheerfully with the rats they have caught in the trenches.

Nine million pigs were slaughtered during the German potato shortage. Here a pig is butchered on the Western Front in 1915 whilst soldiers look on.

Maimed soldiers instructed in beekeeping as an alternative form of employment, via a scheme of Lord Eglington in 1916. The top photograph shows soldiers in uniform in July 1916 being trained in how to smoke the hives prior to opening; the latter shows men examining combs.

With horses already in short supply, circus elephants in both Germany and Britain were requisitioned or borrowed for heavier war work. Here in 1915, an elephant moves logs in Hamburg, under the supervision of German soldiers.

Lizzie, a circus elephant turned munitions worker in Sheffield, pictured in *The Illustrated War News* in February 1916.

A rare European bison, hunted to extinction in the wild by Germans occupying Poland.

A herd of bison in the ancient Białowieża Forest, scattering from the blast of a shell.

A cow forms part of the civilian exodus pulling a refugees' cart from Ypres, Belgium in November 1914.

The cat mascot of a big-gun crew on the Western Front; this maybe a depiction of Lieutenant Lekeux's life-saving cat Pitoutchi.

Chapter 5

A political animal: Use as symbols and propaganda

A wide variety of creatures were utilised by both sides in the First World War as a powerful form of visual currency to express certain ideas, using them symbolically as visual propaganda. Animals could be shorthand for certain qualities (for example bravery being represented by the lion), or serve as symbols of the different nations at war. Depending on who was behind the image, Germany could be portrayed as a snarling boar or a wily dachshund, whilst Britain could be a fierce bulldog or a fat, manipulative spider.

When America entered the war in 1917, two specific types of dog were deployed on a recruitment poster for the US marines. A grim-faced 'devil dog' sporting a Marine's helmet is shown in hot pursuit of a dachshund in a pickelhaube. In a possibly apocryphal story, the Marines allegedly took their 'devil dog' nickname from German descriptions of their ferocity when they joined the First World War, likening them to 'hounds from hell'. Also aiding recruitment was a rather unusual image produced by the publication *Swain's Quarterly*, and posted in their office window located on Shoe Lane, close to Fleet Street, in the City of London. A dachshund, attired in a zeppelin costume for the avoidance of doubt over its allegiance, is pursued by a French poodle, a British bulldog, a Russian borzoi, a Belgian griffon and an Italian greyhound, whilst an officer beckons insistently towards the viewer. The success of the image as a recruitment tool is hard to gauge, but it's certainly eye catching, and *Swain's Quarterly* were sufficiently pleased with it to reproduce it again in their summer 1916 issue.

Though often employed in humorous illustrations, the Teutonic associations of the dachshund resulted in a decline in its popularity as a breed, as patriotic dog lovers of the allied nations choose to express their allegiance through their choice of pet. Attempts were made to rebrand the breed, with the American Kennel Club officially renaming it the 'badger dog' (a literal translation from the German), with others giving it the moniker 'liberty pup'. German shepherd dogs received a similar treatment, and are still known today by some as 'Alsatians', a label given in an attempt to emphasise the French origins of the breed from Alsace, rather than from neighbouring Germany.

Depictions of particular breeds of dogs to illustrate national allegiance was a simple but effective visual tool. The artist Wallace Robinson takes this one step further by attiring these dogs in the military uniforms of their associated country on a postcard in 1915. The American bulldog here is used to suggest to the viewer that America's then neutrality was not to be mistaken for weakness or cowardice.

In an illustration by the celebrated war artist, Fortunino Matania, German soldiers are depicted in Belgium at the Place du Marche, Liege in August 1914, at the very start of the war. In the foreground, a German soldier is shown about to kick a cowering dog, who is transporting bread to the market. In the background, soldiers search the pockets of a civilian, while others loot market produce. Whether animal cruelty genuinely occurred at this incident or if it was just used as an artistic device to project the thuggish nature of the enemy, the treatment of animals could be used as an indicator of character.

On the home front too, depictions of animals were being used to highlight and curtail undesirable behaviour. A British bulldog, depicted turning its head away from a foaming tankard, was enlisted as a symbol of Britain on the front cover of *The Tatler* to illustrate the government's plans to reduce the drinking of alcohol during the First World War. The consumption of alcohol during wartime is suggested by this image to be unpatriotic, with drink hampering the war effort and the production of munitions. Chiming in with the words of David Lloyd-George, then Chancellor of the Exchequer and later Prime Minister, 'We are fighting the Germans, Austrians and drink, and as far as I can see, the greatest of those foes is drink.'

Combining the symbolism of animals with the disarming power of humour was perhaps a surprisingly effective way of getting a message across to an audience. The image of the British bulldog is humorously combined with the introduction of tanks in 1917 in one topical postcard, and in an advert for Bovril, a popular wartime meat extract made from beef, one British bull selflessly offered itself at a recruiting station declaring '*My* place is at the front'. Another striking image allying puns with propaganda is a photograph of Methuselah, a tortoise at London Zoo, that appeared in *The Sketch* in July 1915. Written on both sides of his shell is a patriotic slogan to remind visitors of the need for shells as munitions to aid the war effort: 'We can't do without our shells; but they will serve to remind you that there are others – which your country needs.'

A single creature could be suggestive of several different attributes, depending on the way in which it was portrayed. Louis Wain used his trademark anthropomorphised feline to depict the Kaiser as a slightly ridiculous moustachioed cat on the rampage, brandishing a sword amidst shellfire. Cats could symbolise ferocity, for example as used on a US tanks recruitment poster, as well as good luck, where in a French illustration a black cat is chosen to chase German soldiers out of France.

When selecting creatures to represent the enemy, less appealing animals were chosen. In a German view from 1915 of the *Entente Cordiale* (an Anglo-French agreement encouraging greater cooperation between these two nations from 1904), Britain is depicted as an enormous hairy spider, with its web of influence spreading across Europe. One German poster by Maximilian Lenz promotes the sale of war bonds, using a fire-breathing dragon as a symbol for the Allies. In a 1917 illustration from the German satirical publication *Simplicissimus*, Germany is depicted as an armour-clad knight, saving the world from the evil clutches of the British, who are portrayed in the form of a grasping octopus, its tentacles being steadily lopped off by Germany's sword. Britain is once more satirised in a German illustration of February 1915, depicted as a goggle-eyed duplicitous chameleon, masquerading under the similar looking flag of the Norwegian navy, for fear of U-boats attacks.

The Allies responded in kind in their portrayal of Germany. Germany is depicted as a wild boar, complete with miniature pickelhaube, with its snout caught in a trap labelled 'Verdun'; acting as a British comment in *Punch* magazine in May 1916 on the Germany advance being held at Verdun. The Kaiser and his son the Crown Prince were depicted as bloodthirsty vultures in one French illustration from July 1915. The dove is used as a symbol of peace in a French illustration from February 1917, except behind the mask lies Kaiser Wilhelm II, poised with a bloodstained dagger. A French illustration uses animals to depict the might of the Italian army: against the backdrop of an Italian flag, an Italian light infantryman (Bersaglieri) holds the Imperial German eagle upside, as its crown falls to the ground, whilst an Italian she-wolf eagerly takes a swipe at the bird with one of her paws.

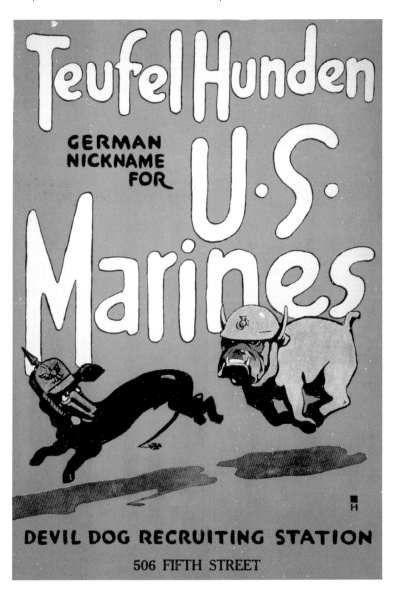

A recruitment poster for the US Marines using dogs as a shorthand for national identity.

HOW WE HELPED RECRUITING.

A Painting by a Swain Artist
in our windows at Shoe Lane.

A curious recruitment image reproduced in the magazine *Swain's Quarterly* in summer 1916. A cavalcade of dogs, each breed symbolising one of the Allies, are depicted cheerfully chasing a dachshund in a zeppelin outfit, symbolising Germany.

English Bulldog   German Dachshund   American Bull Terrier   French Bulldog   Russian Wolf Hound

I'm Neutral, BUT–Not Afraid
of any of them.

Dogs in soldier's uniforms are used to make a political point about America's neutrality in this 1915 illustration by Wallace Robinson.

An illustration that featured in an American publication on Independence Day 1918, using the dachshund to symbolise the German threat.

Entitled 'The dog that nobody will know', this illustration shows an anthropomorphised downcast dachshund being shunned by a British bulldog and French poodle.

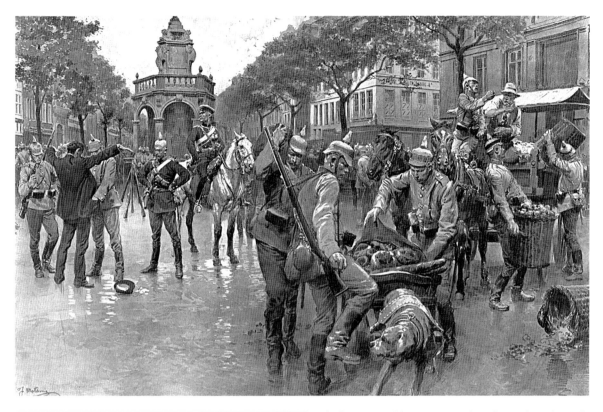

A German soldier portrayed as thuggish and cruel, poised to kick a cowering dog.

A patriotic image of a British bulldog is used to encourage abstinence from alcohol during wartime.

Originally entitled 'No tanks!', this 1917 postcard portrays the recently invented British tank combined with a British bulldog, emphasising the nationality of this new technology.

This patriotic British bull offers itself at a recruiting station.

British Bull :—

"*My* place is at the front—

"I hear they
"want more
"BOVRIL"

BRITISH TO THE BACKBONE

Methuselah, a tortoise at London Zoo, reminds visitors of the need for shells as munitions to aid the war effort, in July 1915.

German soldiers are shown being chased out of France by a lucky black cat.

Louis Wain uses his trademark anthropomorphised feline to depict the Kaiser as a rampaging cat, brandishing a sword amidst shellfire.

A ferocious cat is employed on this recruitment poster for the United States Tanks Corps in 1917.

A fierce American bald eagle backs up Uncle Sam in this US recruitment poster.

The strength and power of the British Empire is symbolised by a pride of lions in this 1915 recruitment poster.

Regiments sometimes selected their mascots as a symbol of the nationality, seen in this choice of a kangaroo as a mascot for Australian troops.

This cheery watercolour was reproduced as a postcard and entitled 'Australia will be there': here Australian soldiers are saluted by a march past of Aussie creatures, including a koala and a kookaburra.

L'ENTENTE CORDIALE

A German view of *L'Entente Cordiale* in 1915, in which Britain is depicted as an enormous hairy spider, with only the Imperial German eagle and her U-boats able to break Britain's malevolent web of influence spreading across Europe and beyond.

A German poster by Maximilian Lenz promotes the sale of war bonds, using a fire-breathing dragon as a symbol for the Allies.

Germany is again depicted doing battle with a terrible beast; here Britain is portrayed as a grasping octopus, taking over the world.

Germany as a wild boar, with its snout caught in a trap labelled 'Verdun'. A British comment in *Punch* magazine in May 1916 on the German advance being held at Verdun.

Britain is depicted in this German illustration at the start of the war as a goggle-eyed duplicitous chameleon, masquerading under the similar looking flag of the Norwegian navy, for fear of U-boats attacks.

The Kaiser and his son the Crown Prince are portrayed as bloodthirsty vultures in this French illustration from July 1915.

LA BAÏONNETTE

LA PAIX ALLEMANDE

DESSINS DE

CAPPIELLO, IRIBE, DEGASTYNE, LEROY, MEUNIER, MÉTIVET, NEUMONT, etc. Texte de JACQUES CONSTANT. Chanson inédite de JEAN BASTIA

The dove is used as a symbol of peace in this French illustration from February 1917, except behind the mask lies Kaiser Wilhelm II, poised with a bloodstained dagger.

A French illustration depicting the might of the Italian army: against the backdrop of an Italian flag, an Italian light infantryman (Bersaglieri) holds the Imperial German eagle upside, as its crown falls to the ground, whilst an Italian she-wolf eagerly takes a swipe at the bird with one of her paws.

Chapter 6

Four-footed fighters: Horses at war

Writing in *The Graphic* in August 1917, William Scarth Dixon, a well-established equine authority put the case forward for the value of the horse in warfare:

> *That horses are taking a bigger part in this war, though not so showy a one as has obtained in previous wars, is made evident by the fact that the Army Establishment requires 900,000 to a million horses. What are they used for? it may well be asked. And the answer may well be: for everything.*

With the great demand for army horses, civilians and organisations alike found their animals being commandeered for the war effort. Two images appeared in *The Illustrated Sporting and Dramatic News* in August 1914, not long after the outbreak of war, showing two different views of horses being requisitioned. A sentimental illustration by Dudley Tennant of a woman bidding farewell to her horse contrasts with a photograph of a soldier leading railway horses (where they were employed for light shunting and delivery of goods) away from their stables at Bexhill in East Sussex.

Where shellfire and mud made roads impassable to mechanised traffic, the horse was invaluable as a means of transport. The great demand for horses and mules for the war effort meant that there was a strong incentive to utilise even the most recalcitrant steeds. Lieutenant Mike Rimington, previously of the 37th Lancers, was one of the 'horse whisperers' charged with breaking in unruly and vicious horses for the British Army. Rimington is pictured at work at the Underdale Hall Remount Department near Shrewsbury, in a spread in *The Illustrated Sporting and Dramatic News* in June 1916. Rimington is photographed with his dog mascot 'Tiger', reclining on the ground with the horses he has tamed standing docilely about him. The horses pictured include 'Savage Simon' whose report from the War Office had described him as 'Vicious and quite unmanageable. Has injured six men, some badly. Savaged the rough-rider and tore the saddle to pieces.' Rimington is also pictured demonstrating how he teaches a horse not to strike a man with 'Bucking Belle', who was previously, 'vicious in stable to handle; kicks when approaching; bucks viciously when mounting'. He is shown standing upright on the saddle of 'Winston Churchill' who was labelled as 'quite unmanageable; very wild in stable; dangerous rearer', and pictured sitting on an obedient-looking 'Cunning Cuss' who was, 'extremely nervous to approach in stall; fed from other stall; rears up and strikes if you attempt to bridle him; refuses and bucks when leaving stable; proved vicious on several occasions'. Another horse tamed by Rimington, the sinisterly named 'Crippen', had previously 'struck out and killed a groom.' Clearly an subject of interest in the press, *The Graphic* also ran a feature on Rimington taming unruly steeds for the war effort a few months later in October 1916, entitled *A Borstal for Bucephalus: how four-footed army outlaws are reclaimed,* where the horses are pictured gathered round a gramophone to listen as part of their treatment.

The important work of the Army Remounts Depot continued on the home front, sourcing horses from all over the country to supply the war effort. Cecil Aldin, sporting illustrator and contributor to many illustrated periodicals including *The Illustrated London News,* became a Remounts Purchasing Officer in Berkshire, responsible for buying horses for war purposes. Travelling up to sixty miles a day, Aldin worked tirelessly to secure the quota of horses required of him by the War Office, as well as managing their care, conditioning and stabling. Though the demands of war reduced Aldin's artistic output, one particular sketch, which was made as a precursor to his portrait of the same scene for the Imperial War Museum, shows women at work at one of the Army Remount Depots under his command. Aldin was notable for his pioneering employment of women, who rose to the challenge of managing even the most difficult horses, with more and more of his depots being put under all-female control.

One unusual contribution of the horse to the war effort was as a supply of serum that acted as an antidote to tetanus poisoning, also known as lockjaw. The tetanus germ is present in the soil and, as it rarely penetrates deep enough beneath the skin, is usually harmless. In wartime however, there is much greater opportunity for a soldier to come into contact with it, due to muddy conditions and open wounds. An article from *The Graphic* in November 1915 relates how serum, or blood fluid with the clotting agents removed, was collected from the blood of specially selected horses, who had been carefully infected with the disease, and had built up an immunity to it. As much as eight or ten quarts (up to an impressive twenty pints) could be taken from a horse at one time, and once the fluid had been prepared, tested and sterilised, it was sealed in glass tubes the size of a little finger, and sent to the front. The Lister Institute of Preventative Medicine had a horse farm at Elstree before the war, but anticipating the increased need, built up the supply of 'serum horses' until there were twenty times the stock as in peacetime. 'The regiment of healing horses… supplies antidotes to diphtheria and dysentery; and it is no exaggeration to say that the blood the horses have shed has saved thousands of lives.' The author is keen to point out that the 'serum horses' live long lives, away from the front lines of battle, and are in the best of health. Their only possible complaint is the monotony of isolation in their stables while the treatment is in progress.

Outside the serum stables, horses on the battlegrounds lived a very different life. With the introduction of gas warfare in 1915, soldiers were trained in the usage of gas masks at centres in England, before being sent to the front. Here men and horses are pictured wearing gas masks at a military efficiency competition at Aldershot in 1917. The threat of poison gas attacks were not the only hazard facing horses at war; the difficult living conditions on the front lines left them vulnerable to disease. One photograph shows five horses treated for mange (infestation of a burrowing mite) by sulphurous acid gas at the veterinary hospital in Abbeville, in the Somme region of northern France. The therapeutic application of gas here is in marked contrast to its use in chemical warfare. At the Blue Cross hospital at Meaux, just north east of Paris, special facilities were constructed for the treatment of mange in horses, this time via special sulphur baths, rather than by gas. A sloping approach lead to a long bath, 50ft long by 4ft wide, which the horses swam along, whilst buckets of warm sulphur solution were thrown over their head and shoulders at intervals as they passed along. The horses went to a large heated shed, where they remained for half an hour whilst the sulphur dried. Two or, at the most, three dippings in this way effected a cure.

Horses and men suffered alike in poor living conditions on the front lines. Good stabling was often found wanting, with men having to make the best of whatever came to hand to accommodate their horses. The skeletal horses being groomed and fed in a muddy, makeshift shelter in the open air circa 1916, gives a taster of what some animals endured, despite the best efforts of the men. The Army Veterinary Corps did much to improve animal welfare, a primary concern being the provision of adequate hospital housing. A chance encounter between the Director of Veterinary Services, Major-General Sir John Moore, and a circus owner stranded in the Gournay district in Normandy, lead to the purchase of a large round circus tent and several horse tents. These were erected in a chalk pit near Abbeville and gave good service for nearly two years; so satisfactory were they that similar tents were ordered from the same manufacturer in Paris and erected at other centres.

One desperate plea came from the RSPCA for their fund for sick and wounded horses. 'Have you given a thought to the horses at the front? They are almost as necessary as men. They bring up the artillery; they bring up supplies. They are essential for mounted troops. They suffer, when wounded, as much as the men… Will you help the horses?' The plea was featured in *The Graphic* in February 1916, barely six months after war began, and reproduced in many other publications to harness support for the work of the RSPCA in wartime.

In one illustration by Richard Caton Woodville Jr., men of the Mounted Section of the Canadian Veterinary Corps are pictured collecting wounded horses in an ambulance from the battlefield in 1916, where they have been in the line of fire from the field artillery. An animal wounded in one of its forelegs is shown being assisted to the ambulance wagon by four men supporting it with a blanket under its belly, while another man leads it. Horses were given first aid, then taken on to a Base Veterinary Hospital, where, if they were deemed to be too severely wounded, they were humanely put out of their misery.

The drawing entitled 'An ordeal of equine nerves' by Howard K. Elcock was featured in *The Graphic* in August 1917, and depicts the dangers of the back areas of the battle zone, even away from the front lines, and illustrates in the chaos that is unleashed when a bomb explodes over a line of horses. The damaging psychological effect on the horses through their continued exposure to the barrage of the guns can be imagined when observing Elcock's drawing. The devastation that a single shell could wreak is bleakly summarised in the image entitled '*Wiped out by a single shell: a holocaust of horses in the danger zone*' by Frank Dadd. The drawing was reproduced in *The Graphic* in June 1917, accompanied by this extract from a machine gun officer's diary:

A little way up the road we came upon a General Service waggon[sic], with a team of horses lying dead beside it. A shell had exploded in the midst of them, killing the lot at once. The drivers, who were about to mount, escaped unhurt. A little way in front another horse lay across the road badly wounded, and had to be shot by one of the men. The waggon was returning after taking supplies to the trenches.

An astute comment on the loss of so many horses' lives in the war comes from the French satirical publication *La Bainonette* in August 1918. The illustration, translated from the French as *Those lost in the war*, reflects an awareness that even whilst the war was being fought, the sacrifice of animal lives had been significant. With slaughter on such an unprecedented scale, it may well be wondered at how the carcasses of so many horses were disposed of over the years. The response to this problem was the establishment of seven 'Horse Carcass Economiser' units, which were linked to veterinary hospitals. Though perhaps a distasteful concept to modern minds, the bodies of dead horses still offered a valuable resource and steady income stream for the army, with suitable specimens being processed and sold to provide horse meat, with the hair, hooves and bones being sold separately by weight.

A spread entitled 'The strange career of our army horses' is featured in *The Graphic* in January 1915, not even six months after the outbreak of war, gives an idea of how even in the early stages of the war, horses were being invalided out of the conflict. A scene at a Blue Cross horse hospital in France is contrasted with the fate of those British army horses deemed unfit for future military service: to be sold on to French farmers. For those men and horses who survived the war, demobilisation meant a parting of the ways, with horses being sold off at auction. The bond between man and horse, who had experienced so much together, could be strong. In one Canadian official photograph, reproduced in *The Sphere* in March 1919, a Canadian staff officer in France 'shakes hands' with his horse, as he bids it farewell. Fortunino Matania's famous painting *Goodbye, Old Man* was a moving depiction of a soldier bidding farewell to his dying horse. Painted to raise money for the Blue Cross, an organisation dedicated to improving animal welfare, the picture was extremely popular, with prints and postcards being sold in abundance.

There are many stories of individual horses and the companionship they shared with soldiers during the war. A German pony found by the men of 2nd Battalion of the King's Royal Rifles was adopted as a mascot and named 'Coal Box'. Coal Box was cared for by Lance-Corporal Geary of the Band, which he accompanied on parade, marching at the head of the Battalion, except on long marches, when the Quartermaster reportedly provided a special box on the back of a lorry. Remarkably, Coal Box survived the war, though when he arrived in Portsmouth after hostilities had ceased, he was nearly blind in one eye. By the time the battalion was posted to Ireland, Coal Box's other eye was deteriorating too, and it was decided to put him out of his misery. However, the memory of loyal Coal Box lives on, as one of his hooves was polished, silver plated and engraved with the words 'Coal Box 1914-1920', and is kept in The Royal Green Jackets (Rifles) Museum in Winchester, along with Coal box's chestnut hide.

As horses were loyal to their men, men were loyal to their horses. Two soldiers risked their lives to free two trapped horses, returning them uninjured to British lines in Gallipoli, after a fierce bombardment by the Turks. An officer who was an eyewitness recalls:

> ...a four-horsed waggon[sic] containing poles for telegraphic purposes was coming over the hill, and just as it got to the crest a shell dropped near the waggon, badly damaging it and killing two of the horses. There were, however, still two horses left, and as the shaft pole was now sticking up at an angle the Turks evidently took it to be a gun and began dropping shells at a rate of four a minute. The horses seemed to possess a charmed life. Shell after shell dropped. It seemed impossible that they could live. Then through my glasses I could see two men trying to cut the animals loose. When they heard a shell coming I saw one man take cover behind a tree, and the other get behind the waggon. A few minutes later they galloped the horses bareback past our trenches amid cheers from their friends. They were two men of the 1st Royal Munster Fusiliers. They both received their promotion that evening.

'The Old Blacks' were a team of gun horses, originally attached to F Battery of the Royal Horse Artillery, who remarkably served together throughout the war, and returned home to their old pre-war stalls in St John's Wood Barracks once the war was over. Serving with the original British Expeditionary Force in France in 1914, the horses changed hands many times, with their names being cheerfully changed to match the initial of each of the batteries they served. So when with J battery, the horses were dubbed 'Jubb', 'Jabber', 'Ju-Jitsu' and 'Job-master', only to be re-christened 'Not 'alf' and 'Naughty' whilst under the aegis of N Battery. After seeing much action, they returned to England in 1919, where they participated in the funerals of many notable people. The horses were selected to pull the gun carriage bearing the remains of the unknown warrior on 11 November 1920, and are pictured later in this chapter parading at St John's Wood Barracks before the burial at Westminster Abbey.

'Ragtime', also known as 'Raggie', was a grey Arab horse, photographed with his five medals displayed on his brow band. Three were for service during the First World War, one for the Arab Revolt, and one for long service and good conduct. Born at a regimental farm in India in 1910, Ragtime served in Mesopotamia with the cavalry under his master Michael Willoughby, the 11th Baron Middleton. In summer 1916, they parted company, with Lord Middleton returning to India, and Raggie being sold to the government, going to a horse depot. After the Armistice, they were fortuitously reunited with at a polo match in Baghdad. In January 1924, Raggie was sent to Birdsall House, Lord Middleton's Yorkshire seat, where he lived a well-earned life of comfort and ease. Once a year, he travelled to York to collect charitable donations on behalf of horses and other animals in need.

Creatures born on active service were for some a sign of hope, and a reminder that even amidst the destruction and chaos of the war, the natural order continued undeterred. When a foal was born at the time of the battle of Vimy Ridge, near Arras, in France in 1917, it was named 'Vimy', in honour of its birth place, and was pictured with its mother in a Canadian official war photograph.

A sentimental depiction of a woman bidding farewell to her horse, requisitioned for the war effort.

A soldier leading a railway horse away from stables at Bexhill in August 1914.

Lieutenant Mike Rimington, previously of the 37th Lancers, was one of the 'horse whisperers' charged with breaking in unruly and vicious horses for the British Army.

Rimington artfully remains in the saddle as a horse rears.

by Lieutenant Rimington. Clockwise from top left: 'Savage Simon (seen in the extreme left of the picture)', 'Bucking Belle', Rimington standing on the back of 'Winston Churchill' and 'Cunning Cuss' is pictured before and after treatment.

Lt. Rimington (with his mascot "Tiger"), among horses who were a few days previously vicious kickers and strikers. "Savage Simon" stands peaceably on the extreme left of the picture.

A test for horses before issuing them to the troops. Teaching "Bucking Belle" not to strike at a fallen man.

Teaching "Cunning Cuss" not to strike.—Before treatment this horse was vicious, and struck and kicked when approached.

"Cunning Cuss" when cured and educated. It should be noted that other horses were loose in the field at the time of taking photo.

"Winston Churchill" completely cured by the Lieutenant.

A SUCCESSFUL BREAKER AND TEACHER OF ARMY HORSES.

The horses gather round a gramophone to listen as part of their treatment.

A sketch made by the artist and Remounts Purchasing Officer Cecil Aldin, showing women at work in one of his Army Remount Depots.

A regiment of healing horses at Elstree in Essex, responsible for the supply of tetanus serum.

Men and horses wearing gas masks at a military efficient competition at Aldershot in 1917.

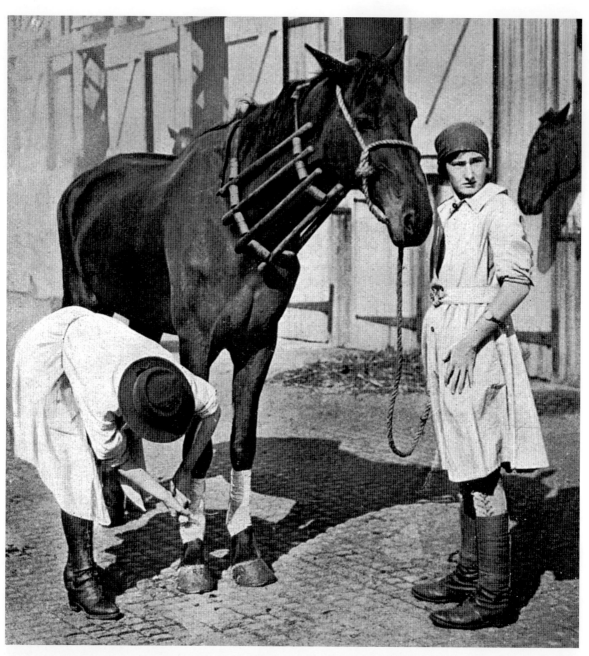

A female vet minsters unto a sick horse at an English horse repository in 1917.

A vet tends to a wounded horse hit by shrapnel in France, circa 1916.

A trio of pictures that appeared in *The Graphic* in 1917, showing the difficult working conditions that horses on the front lines had to endure.

MUDDLING THROUGH THE MUD OF FLANDERS
RECENT BRITISH OFFICIAL PHOTOGRAPHS FROM THE WESTERN FRONT

Five horses treated for mange using sulphurous acid gas.

Skeletal horses being groomed and fed in a muddy, makeshift shelter in the open air circa 1916.

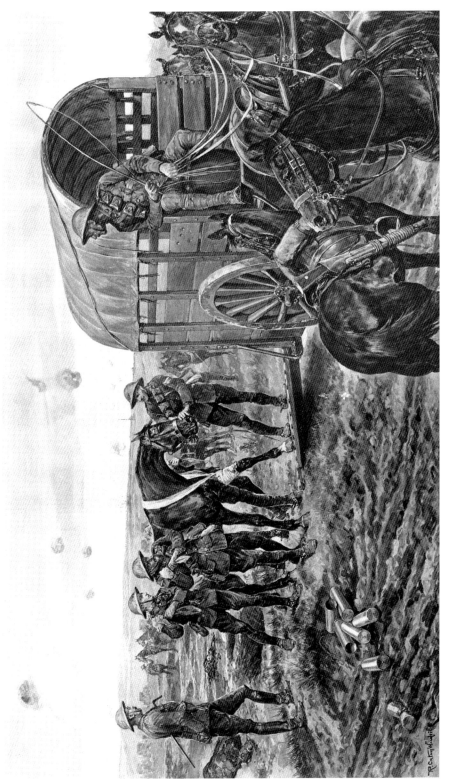

Men of the Mounted Section of the Canadian Veterinary Corps collecting wounded horses in an ambulance from the battlefield in 1916.

The chaos that is unleashed when a bomb explodes over a line of horses.

'Wiped out by a single shell: a holocaust of horses in the danger zone' by Frank Dadd.

Those lost in the war. French commentary in 1918 on the massive death toll of horses during the war.

HAVE YOU GIVEN A THOUGHT
TO THE HORSES AT THE FRONT ?

They are almost as necessary as men.
They bring up the artillery ; they bring up supplies.
They are essential for mounted troops.
And they suffer, when wounded, as much as men.

Your Heart goes out in Sympathy for their Misery and Pain.

HOW CAN YOU HELP THEM ?

BY SUPPORTING

THE R.S.P.C.A. FUND
for Sick and Wounded Horses,

The only organisation approved by Army Council
as an auxiliary to the Army Veterinary Corps.

The R.S.P.C.A. FUND is erecting in France a hospital for **1,000** horses, with recreation rooms, etc., for the men.

The R.S P.C.A. FUND has supplied six horse ambulances for the front, and is sending six more.

The R.S.P.C.A. FUND has ordered, and will shortly be despatching to the front, a number of motor lorries for conveying forage from the stations, etc., as well as corn crushers and chaff cutters with petrol engines complete, for use at each of the Hospitals.

The R.S.P.C.A. FUND is building a shelter for **500** horses, where first-aid treatment can be given.

The R.S.P.C.A. FUND has sent out large consignments of rugs, halters, bandages, etc.

The R.S.P.C.A. FUND has trained, and sent to the A.V.C. for enlistment, nearly **200** competent men to serve in the Hospitals.

WILL YOU HELP
THE HORSES ?

Cheques and postal orders (*crossed " Coutts & Co."*) should be sent to—
E. G. FAIRHOLME, *Hon. Sec. of the Fund,*
105, Jermyn Street, London, S.W.

A plea from the Royal Society for the Prevention of Cruelty to Animals for their fund for sick and wounded horses.

Poster circa 1916 to raise funds for the Blue Cross.

AMONG FRIENDS — A BLUE CROSS HOSPITAL IN FRANCE, WHERE OUR WOUNDED AND WAR-WORN HORSES ARE TENDED

AMONG FOREIGNERS — FRENCH FARMERS BUYING BRITISH ARMY HORSES WHICH ARE UNFIT FOR FURTHER MILITARY SERVICE

'The strange career of our army horses': a page from The Graphic in January 1915, showing wounded horses being cared for at a Blue Cross hospital in France, with a contrasting picture beneath of French farmers buying up horses who were judged unfit for further military service.

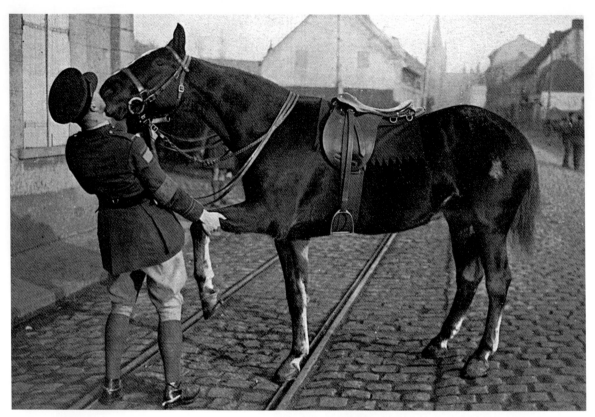

A Canadian staff officer bids farewell to his horse after being demobbed.

Fortunino Matania's famous painting portraying a soldier bidding farewell to his dying horse, entitled *Goodbye, Old Man.*

A soldier with the pony mascot Coal Box of the King's Royal Rifles, pictured in France circa 1916.

Two soldiers risk their lives to free two horses trapped in a shelled wagon.

'The Old Blacks' parading at St John's Wood Barracks before the burial of the unknown warrior at Westminster Abbey in 1920.

Ragtime the grey Arab horse displaying his service medals on his brow band.

Vimy the foal of Vimy Ridge, born on active service.

Chapter 7
Mules and donkeys at the front

Though the plight of horses in wartime has been in the public eye with Michael Morpurgo's book, *War Horse*, mules (the offspring of a male donkey and a female horse) and donkeys also played an important role in the war.

Mules have a reputation as being stubborn creatures, and it took experience to train them so they would be fit for military duties. One feature in *The Illustrated Sporting and Dramatic News* in September 1915 depicted the methods of Mr Fred Ginnett, a horse trainer and member of the Ginnett circus family, employed for breaking-in mules for the army. The original caption reports that he was assisted by several Mexican boys, who are described as being proficient with the lasso.

The logistics of transporting mules and donkeys once they were deemed fit for service was considerable. The war artist Fortunino Matania illustrated for *The Sphere* a mule intended for transporting artillery equipment being hoisted precariously via a sling onto a ledge on the Italian front in the Alps in July 1915.

Donkeys formed an important part of the supply chain, delivering food and other requisites to where they were needed on the front lines. Their size enabled them to pick their way along the path of a trench, delivering supplies. They were employed as beasts of burden with many images showing their muddy plight in the press. Though mules were thought to be more sure-footed than horses, the churned-up mud of the front lines still presented a hazard for them. Soldiers' diaries record animals slipping off the poorly kept roads, and becoming so deeply stuck in the mud that rescue was impossible. One grim solution was to shoot them, and then as many as three men would stand on the corpses to sink them beneath the surface of the mud in lieu of a burial.

The sheer surface area of larger creatures such as mules and horses meant that they were more vulnerable to flying shrapnel. A British army vet was photographed holding a 14oz time fuse, which he pulled from the mule's head. The terrible moment a mule is struck by a shell splinter during the Battle of the Drocourt-Quéant Line in September 1918 at Remy, France is caught on camera. Its rider looks on aghast as the mule falls whilst in harness, whilst the limber (a two wheeled cart, often used to transport artillery) that it was pulling with five other mules ploughs into it from behind. With the loss of the pulling power of one mule, the transporting of the load would become more difficult, and the ensuing uncoupling of the mule would leave the men and remaining mules vulnerable to stray bullets or targeted attack from the enemy. As with horses, the loss of life of these creatures was immense.

Whilst these wounded mules and donkeys suffered greatly, a fortunate few were enthusiastically adopted as regimental pets, and treated with great love and kindness. When the 26th Divisional Train in Salonika found a small donkey dying by the roadside, they adopted it as their mascot and named it Tiny. The *Illustrated Sporting and Dramatic News* featured a picture of Tiny in January 1916, reporting that he 'has since used his liberty by breaking every known written or unwritten military law in the camp. He has also been known to drink nine mugs of tea in succession.'

Another rescued donkey was Jimmy, who became the mascot of the Royal Scots. Accounts differ as to the circumstances of Jimmy's birth, but it's believed that he was born during the Battle of the Somme in 1916 and, his mother having died, was raised by the soldiers of the regiment on tins of condensed milk. Jimmy the donkey was taught to raise his hoof in salute and could beg on his hind legs for his favourite treat of biscuits spread with jam. Wounded several times, Jimmy served by carrying supplies, ammunition and wounded men, being promoted to corporal for his efforts, and wearing his chevrons of rank on his harness. When the war was over, Jimmy was sent to the Remount Depot at Swaythling in Hampshire, where he was sold to a Peterborough dealer. Mrs Heath, the local secretary to the RSPCA, felt that Jimmy deserved a good home after his wartime experiences, and starting a 'shilling fund' to purchase him at public auction. Mrs Heath even went to the trouble and expense of having Jimmy x-rayed, to check for hidden shrapnel in his wounds. Jimmy became the mascot of the Peterborough branch of the RSPCA, and lived there until his death in 1943. Wearing his brow band with four wounded stripes on, Jimmy went on to raise considerable sums in aid of the RSPCA in his civilian life, with the help of two cavalry wallets on his back to collect the donations in. Peter Shaw Baker in his book *Animal War Heroes* related a moving post-war tale about Jimmy:

> One day when Jimmy was collecting in the Peterborough Cattle Market, on the Roll of Honour Flag Day, a soldier, Dudley by name, who had served with the Cameronians in France, happened to be in Peterborough that day, and was amazed to see the former mascot of his regiment. The donkey seemed to recognise his old army pal, for he immediately saluted him with a kiss. Private Dudley had served throughout the war, and had known Jimmy ever since he was born.

In addition to their role as transportation, animals had an enormous capacity for bringing cheer and boosting morale. Donkeys were used to give convalescing soldiers rides or drives, bringing much needed diversion, entertainment and joy, particularly to those rendered immobile by their injuries. King George V is pictured in 1917 stroking one of the donkeys at the Royal Victoria Military Hospital at Netley, near Southampton, which had been expanded and used by the Red Cross to treat around 50,000 patients during the First World War.

A captured German donkey is used as a form of visual joke in an official photograph, taken somewhere on the Cambrai front in France and featured in *The Graphic* in December 1917. The image is captioned 'The indestructible humour of Mr. Atkins: A new use for the pickelhaube. A captured donkey decorated with the proud Prussian helmet and led in triumph'. The British soldier was sometimes referred to as 'Tommy Atkins', and an appetite for japes, even in the thick of war, is well illustrated by this photograph. That the enemy's animals, as well as their other supplies, could be captured and re-purposed, is shown here. The mocking pickelhaube perched between the donkey's ears is a good-humoured gesture, but also suggests the enemy as an ass: foolish and stubborn. The glee afforded by the opportunity to get one up on the enemy by purloining their property, as well as obtaining souvenirs (such as the ever popular pickelhaube), can be seen on the faces of these soldiers, in much need of the diversion of a good joke.

Donkeys and mules played an essential and sometimes overlooked role in transportation and logistics in the Great War, but also brought much needed companionship and humour.

For their bravery and intelligence, companionship and loyalty in the face of terrible hardship, the contribution of animals in wartime should not be under estimated; all the more because they cannot speak for themselves. These images demonstrate the extent of the debt owed to those faithful creatures.

Donkeys employed as beasts of burden in October 1916 transporting churns of soup held in woven panniers to Maurepas, in the Somme region, to the French front lines.

A mule for transporting artillery equipment being hoisted precariously via a sling onto a ledge on the Italian front in the Alps in July 1915.

How the plight of mules at the front was reported in the press: 'Mules in the mire of the battle area: a tragedy of the Flanders mud in three acts.'

Official photograph   Official photograph   Official photograph
MULES IN THE MIRE OF THE BATTLE AREA: A TRAGEDY OF THE FLANDERS MUD IN THREE ACTS

A mule is struck by a shell splinter during the Battle of the Drocourt-Quéant Line in September 1918 at Remy, France.

A British army vet holding a 14oz time fuse, which he pulled from the mule's head.

The difficult conditions on the front lines: a mule waiting to be shod in a specially constructed frame, circa 1916.

Tiny the donkey rescued and made the mascot of the 26th Divisional train.

Jimmy the donkey, mascot of the 1st Scottish Rifles.

King George V meets one of the donkeys at the Royal Victoria Military Hospital at Netley, near Southampton.

'The indestructible humour of Mr. Atkins: A new use for the pickelhaube. A captured donkey decorated with the proud Prussian helmet and led in triumph.'

'Mr Fred Ginnett, a horse trainer and member of the Ginnett circus family, employed for breaking-in mules for the army. He is assisted by several Mexican boys, who are proficient with the lasso.'

1. The mule quite docile after a severe drilling.
4. Tackling a bucking mule.

2. Throwing a mule with lasso.

3. A mule trying to throw its rider.
5. Securing a mule with the lasso.